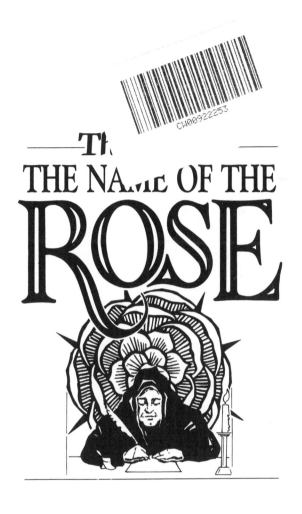

—T

# THE NAME OF THE
# ROSE

Including translations of all non-English passages
Adele J. Haft
Jane G. White
Robert J. White

*Ann Arbor*

THE UNIVERSITY OF MICHIGAN PRESS

2011   2010   2009   2008      11   10   9   8

*A CIP catalog record for this book is available from the British Library.*


Library of Congress Cataloging-in-Publication Data

Haft, Adele J.
    The key to "The name of the rose" : including translations of all
non-English passages / Adele J. Haft, Jane G. White, Robert J.
White.
        p.      cm.
    Includes bibliographical references.
    ISBN 0-472-08621-9 (paper : alk. paper)
    1. Eco, Umberto.   Nome della rosa Concordances.   I. White, Jane
G.   II. White, Robert J., 1939–   .   III. Title.
PQ4865.C6N6347      1999
853'.914—dc21                                          99-29488
                                                          CIP

ISBN 978-0-472-08621-4 (paper : alk. paper)

This book is dedicated to Robert and Lucie Giegengack,
to Myrle Cates Gilles, and to J. K. Martin

# Acknowledgments

We wish to thank for their kind help and constant encouragement the staff of the Bryn Mawr College library and Elizabeth A. Baxter; Frank Gilles; Virginia Gilles Haft and Harold Haft; Bruce Haft; Mark Jupiter; Carol Martin; Nancy Moore; Kathryn Naughton of Harcourt Brace Jovanovich; Christopher Ross; Rev. Patrick J. Ryan, S.J.; Prof. Mary C. Sullivan of Hunter College; and Jordan Zinovich.

Patricia Klein, President of Ampersand Associates, Inc., enabled us to publish the original edition of our *Key to "The Name of the Rose,"* and Thomas Cahill distributed the book through his Cahill and Company Catalogue. We remain grateful to Patricia for bringing our book to life in the United States and Japan, and to Tom for guiding its first steps.

Finally, we thank Ellen Bauerle and Perry Elizabeth Pearson of the University of Michigan Press, who dedicated themselves to reissuing *The Key to "The Name of the Rose."* Their excitement and expertise—coupled with those of the three readers they chose to review our book—mean more to us than we can say.

Adele J. Haft
Jane Giegengack White
Robert J. White

# Contents

# Preface

In his *Postscript to "The Name of the Rose,"* Umberto Eco asks:

> What does it mean, to imagine a reader able to overcome the penitential obstacle of the first hundred pages? It means, precisely, writing one hundred pages for the purpose of constructing a reader suitable for what comes afterward. . . .
>
> What model reader did I want as I was writing? An accomplice, to be sure, one who would play my game. . . . But at the same time, with all my might, I wanted to create a type of reader who, once the initiation was past, would become my prey—or, rather, the prey of the text—and would think he wanted nothing but what the text was offering him. (1984, 48 and 50, 53)

Fifteen years have passed since the three of us—Adele Haft, Jane White, and Robert White—fell prey to Eco's first novel, a stunning *tour de force* about crimes in a medieval abbey and the obsession of its monks with heresies, apocalyptic visions, and forbidden knowledge. Like the characters in Umberto Eco's fictitious monastic library, we already shared a love of books and classical erudition when we stumbled upon the text that became for us, in Eco's words, "an experience of transformation" (*Postscript* 1984, 51).

Different paths led each of us to Eco's best-selling novel. Adele Haft's husband, Jordan Zinovich, a writer himself, not only introduced her to *The Name of the Rose* but convinced her to begin translating and identifying the Latin passages that Eco had scattered throughout his mystery. In the meantime, the Whites first set foot in Eco's octagonal Aedificium when a publisher sent them a review copy of the book. Then, in the spring of 1984, we three found ourselves drawn together by our mutual passion for *The Name of the Rose.* Though long-time colleagues in

the Department of Classical and Oriental Studies at Hunter College of
the City University of New York, the three of us had never before worked
together on a project. To our delight, we soon discovered that each of us
brought complementary skills and interests to our examination of *The
Name of the Rose*. After poring over arcane manuscripts at various research libraries, brainstorming in the halls of Hunter College, collecting
and assembling the hundreds of fragments of our research—we gradually brought our *Key to "The Name of the Rose"* to life.

Originally published in 1987, *The Key to "The Name of the Rose"*
remains the only commentary on Umberto Eco's historical novel available in English. (In his *Postscript to "The Name of the Rose,"* Eco point-
edly refuses to clarify the sources of his quotations and allusions. That
task, he feels, belongs to others like us.) *The Name of the Rose*, arguably
Eco's finest novel, has become a classic. To date, *The Name of the Rose*
has been translated into twenty-two languages, sparking a need for commentaries in other languages. In 1990, Japanese interest in Eco's novel
resulted in our *Key to "The Name of the Rose"* being translated by Isamu
Taniguchi for the publishing house of Jiritsu Shobo. The Japanese edition of *The Key to "The Name of the Rose"* is still in print, and Eco has
pointed to the American version of our *Key* as a model for others writing
non-English guides to *The Name of the Rose*.

Readers continue to enter Eco's mysterious labyrinth for any
number of reasons. Some are lured to *The Name of the Rose* because of a
fascination with the Middle Ages. Others come to *The Name of the Rose*
after tasting Eco's latest novels: *Foucault's Pendulum* and *The Island of the
Day Before*. *Foucault's Pendulum*, published in the United States in 1989,
is set in present-day Paris, Milan, and Brazil. Like *The Name of the Rose*,
it is a vast, erudite detective story. An often comical work about a conspiracy to take over the world by locating and controlling the earth's
Telluric Navel, a point in the planet's hollow center that is also the exact center of the sky, it displays its author's encyclopedic knowledge of
subjects ranging from pre-Celtic Stonehenge and the medieval Knights
Templar to nineteenth-century physics (Jean Bernard Léon Foucault,
the inventor of a swinging pendulum designed to demonstrate the axial
rotation of the earth) and twentieth-century pop culture (Woody Allen,
Captain Marvel, Mickey Mouse, and the Beatles).

No less challenging, complex, or richly rewarding, *The Island of
the Day Before*, published six years later, recounts the adventures of
Roberto della Griva, a young Milanese nobleman who is tossed over-

board by a violent storm at sea but eventually saves himself by climbing onto another vessel that has been mysteriously abandoned one mile west of a South Pacific island. Unable to swim, Roberto becomes "shipwrecked" on the deserted ship. Eco takes advantage of his hero's sojourn on the boat to dazzle his readers with a panoramic view of the people and events that shaped seventeenth-century Europe (Cardinal Mazarin and the Thirty Years' War, for example) and to delight them with tantalizing burlesques of Renaissance poetry, especially the love lyrics of Giambattista Marino and John Donne. To parody Renaissance science, moreover, he creates an "Aristotelian Machine"—a bizarre computerlike piece of furniture, with eighty-one drawers and a crank, which is able to generate endless combinations of data—and includes a lengthy pseudo-scientific discourse on the Powder of Sympathy.

Still others have experienced the breathtaking range of Eco's erudition displayed in some of his recent critical works. *The Search for the Perfect Language*, first published in English in 1995, is an endlessly fascinating and exhaustively informative history of mankind's futile attempts to recover or construct the "perfect language." Eco begins with the Book of Genesis (and the language that Adam presumably used to speak to God and name the animals, the "confounding of languages" inflicted on the builders of the Tower of Babel, and the confusing references to the "different tongues" of Noah's sons in chapter 11). He then traces the unattainable quest from the linguistic theories of Raymond Lull, John Wilkins, Athanasius Kircher, and Leibniz to such modern-day IALs (international auxiliary languages) as Volapük, Tutonisch, and Esperanto, the last invented by Ledger Ludwik Zamenhof, a Lithuanian Jew, who believed that his artificial language might end prejudice and promote universal peace.

Uncanny in his ability to straddle "the world of high academe and popular culture" (Scott Sullivan, "Superstar Professor," in *Newsweek*, 29 September 1986, 62), Eco has won admirers even among moviegoers. In 1986, Jean-Jacques Annaud's film version of *The Name of the Rose* enticed many to open the pages of Eco's novel. Now in video, Annaud's film—starring Sean Connery as Brother William, Christian Slater as his young apprentice, and F. Murray Abraham as the inquisitor Bernard Gui—has inspired a new generation to read *The Name of the Rose*.

Whatever has brought or returned you to Eco's masterpiece, our hope is that *The Key to "The Name of the Rose"* will serve as a scholarly but readable companion, one that will enhance your understanding and enjoyment of Eco's intricate text. For those who want to know more about medieval society, *The Key to "The Name of the Rose"* offers a convenient introduction to the general history and climate of the Middle Ages. It is a "Who's Who" of medieval characters, a compilation particularly rich for the period leading up to 1327—the date in which Eco has set *The Name of the Rose.*

By reissuing our book, the University of Michigan Press has fulfilled our dream that *The Key to "The Name of the Rose"* be available to all new readers who find themselves, like us, Eco's willing "accomplices." It is no small miracle that (re)reading *The Name of the Rose* still affects us as terribly and sublimely as it did that first time in 1983.

Adele J. Haft, Jane G. White, Robert J. White
New York City, September 1998

# Authors' Notes

One of the stated purposes of this book is to translate the non-English phrases and words that appear in *The Name of the Rose*. In all but a few instances, a non-English phrase or word is followed directly by its translation. A major exception to this is papal bulls. The titles of papal bulls are the first two or three words of the writing itself; translation gives the reader no new understanding of the meaning of the text. So we have indicated that a writing is indeed a papal bull, but have not provided a translation of the title.

Occasionally we encountered discrepancies in dating a person or event. We have indicated such discrepancies by using a slash between the variant dates. An example is the birth date of Saint Thomas Aquinas, which we have noted as 1224/25.

All references back to the text of *The Name of the Rose* are noted as follows: Eco 341.35/*411.23*. Throughout this book, all page and line numbers from the Harcourt Brace and Company clothbound (1983) and paperbound Harvest (1994) editions of *The Name of the Rose* appear in roman type, and all page and line numbers from the 1984 Warner Books paperbound edition appear in *italic type*.

All quotations from the Bible are from the Authorized King James Version.

And finally, any person or subject whose name appears in boldface type is included in the alphabetical "Annotated Guide to the Historical and Literary References in *The Name of the Rose*" (Chapter 3).

# Introduction

After the American publication in the summer of 1983 of Umberto Eco's *The Name of the Rose*, we found ourselves constantly besieged by overwrought friends who—convinced that Eco had, with malice aforethought, concealed in Latin some of the juicier clues to the murders set in his Benedictine abbey—requested "free translations" of the Latin, especially of *stat rosa pristina nomine, nomina nuda tenemus.* We began our project, therefore, with the intention of translating into English the Latin, French, and German passages in the mystery. But gradually our project grew: as we worked on the translations and began tracking down Eco's sources, we discovered a rich and marvelous maze of literary allusions illuminating not only the basic themes of the novel, but the solution as well.

Eco has created a fictional abbey whose architecture resembles that of several monasteries built in the 13th and 14th centuries and has filled it not only with fictional monks like William of Baskerville, his detective (a combination of Roger Bacon, William of Occam, and Sherlock Holmes) but also with a number of historical figures, such as Ubertino of Casale, Michael of Cesena, and Bernard Gui. Using the logic of William of Occam and St. Thomas Aquinas, William of Baskerville investigates the murders and emerges, in the end, with a solution that reflects the nominalism of Abelard, Occam, and Bernard of Cluny.

Our book is intended as a key—to be used while reading, or rereading, the novel. Chapter One is a short essay on Umberto Eco, his scholarly interests and intellectual biases, on the medieval context of his novel, and on some of the central images and themes that structure *The Name of the Rose.* Next follows a brief chronology of events that relate to the novel. Chapter Three is a glossary of historical and literary references. Arranged alphabetically, these include heresies, mythological allusions, significant events, and biographical sketches of the important and not-so-important people in Eco's story.

Chapter Four contains page-by-page translations of all the non-English passages in the book, including the linguistic hodgepodge of Salvatore. These translations are often accompanied by comments on the literary context and historical background of the references. Throughout, we have tried to avoid any explanations that might give the reader more information than Eco intends him to possess. *The Name of the Rose* is, after all, a mystery.

The final section, or Postscript, is reserved for those who have finished the novel and know the solution. Here we have allowed ourselves a few final comments on the meaning of *The Name of the Rose*.

It would be ideal to have seven consecutive evenings in which to savor *The Name of the Rose*, to unravel with Brother William and Adso the clues surrounding each of the bizarre deaths in Eco's medieval monastery. But whether time in "this aging world" allows you to read *The Name of the Rose* quickly or slowly, once or repeatedly, let our book be a guide through the multi-layered symbolism and a companion through the labyrinthine landscape of Eco's 14th century "underworld."

CHAPTER ONE

# Umberto Eco, Semiotics, and Medieval Thought

For years, Umberto Eco, a respected historian and literary critic, has been Italy's leading expert in semiotics—the study of the different sign systems that men use to communicate to one another. His major works on the subject, *La struttura assente* [The Absent Structure] (1968), *Le forme del contenuto* [The Forms of Content] (1971), and, available in English, *A Theory of Semiotics* (1976), *The Role of the Reader* (1979), and *Semiotics and the Philosophy of Language* (1984), develop a vital body of semiological theory and reveal Eco to be the most original and flamboyant figure in semiotic theory since Roland Barthes. As unofficial spokesman for popular European culture, he has written several engaging studies on the narrative structure of James Bond novels, of Eugène Sue's nineteenth century commercial potboiler *Les Mystères de Paris,* and of comic strips such as Superman, Mandrake the Magician, and Felix the Cat. A man of encyclopedic interests, Eco compiled with G. B. Zorzoli, a nuclear physicist at the Polytechnical Institute in Milan, an absorbing if unconventional chronicle of man's scientific and technical achievements, *The Picture History of Inventions: From Plough to Polaris.*

Two of Eco's most influential works are devoted to aesthetics. In *Opera aperta* [The Open Work] (1962) and *Le poetiche di Joyce: dalla "Summa" al "Finnegans Wake"* [The Poetics of

Joyce: From the 'Summa Theologica' to 'Finnegans Wake']
(1966), Eco examines musical compositions by Stockhausen,
Luciano Berio, and Boulez, the sculptures of Alexander Calder,
French symbolist poetry of the late nineteenth century, and the
novels of James Joyce to show that much of contemporary art is
an "open work," that is, it is radically ambiguous in its message
and invites or, in some cases, compels the reader, listener, or
viewer to participate in the creative process. For example, the
individual performer is given almost unprecedented freedom in
playing the works of, say, Stockhausen or Berio. He is free not
only to interpret the composer's instructions (as he would a tra-
ditional piece of music) but is asked to impose his own judgment
on the actual form of the piece, since it is he who determines
how long he will hold certain notes or in what order he will play
them.

Unlike classical compositions in which the composer ar-
ranges a collection of sound units in a closed, clearly delineated
fashion—one that compels the performer to reproduce the pattern devised by the composer—many modern works eschew the
fixed framework, the "concluded message," in order to multiply
the possibilities of the arrangement of their elements. They are
presented to the performer not as finite works which demand
exact repetition along given structural coordinates, but as "open"
works—intrinsically unfinished, do-it-yourself kits of improvisa-
tional creation.

The *Mobiles* of Alexander Calder and mobile sculptures
by other artists are, similarly, "open" works. By moving in the
air and continuously creating their own space, they discard a
static view of order and set no limit on the number of possible
meanings. Among modern literary texts, moreover, James Joyce's
*Finnegans Wake*, the last sentence of which is incomplete and can
only be finished by turning back to the beginning of the novel,
is, according to Eco, the supreme example of a narrative "open
work."

Now, with the publication of his own "open work," *The
Name of the Rose*, a riveting novel of monks, metaphysics, and

murder set in the Middle Ages, Eco has become internationally famous. The book has sold more than half a million copies in Italy since 1980, has been a huge bestseller in France, and has won three of Europe's most prestigious literary awards—France's Prix Medici, Italy's Premio Strega and Premio Viareggio. In the United States, *The Name of the Rose* has sold over a million copies in hardcover and paperback sales exceeded 800,000 in the first three months.

In many ways, *The Name of the Rose* is precisely the kind of novel one might expect a man with Eco's intellectual interests to write. It is a detective story—what Italians call a *giallo*—and historians and semioticians (along with archaeologists) are Academe's quintessential sleuths. The historian amasses, interprets, and explains his evidence using methods not markedly different from those employed by the fictional detective. Both search for evidence which provides partial answers to their questions, arrange it into meaningful patterns, and evaluate its validity, significance, and causal interrelationships. The detective and historian judge the credibility of their witnesses, be they living persons or texts, in order to determine possible biases that might affect the events being described. Much of their work, moreover, involves a lot of solitary drudgery—drudgery that must be accepted if the clue is not to be lost. The false lead must be pursued to ascertain whether it is, in fact, false; the silent witness must be asked the reason for his silence. Finally, both must make the grand leap from evidence to conclusion—a process that invariably entails an intuition, or "legitimate inference."

Like the detective and the historian, the semiotician, too, lives in a universe of clues. Semiotics is the science of signs, and the semiotician's primary task is to interpret culture as a system of signs. Although the history of semiotic thought extends back through the Middle Ages to the time of Plato and Aristotle, modern semiotics begins with the work of Charles Sanders Peirce and Ferdinand de Saussure. According to both Peirce and de Saussure, cultural artifacts constitute a series of signs, an almost endless chain of relationships from which meaning emerges. Every act of communication is regarded as a message sent and received through different kinds of signs. The complex rules that govern the combination of these messages are prescribed by social codes. All forms of expression—music, art, film, fashion, food, and literature—can be analyzed as a system of signs.

In *A Theory of Semiotics*, Eco enumerates the various branches of semiotics, the seemingly infinite fields of study being investigated by semioticians. There is zoosemiotics, which explores the communicative behavior of non-human communities. By studying how animals exchange information and transmit ideas, the zoosemiotician hopes to discover what the biological components of human communication are. There are semioticians, too, who analyze olfactory signs (from perspiration to perfume), formalized languages (such as algebra, chemistry, Morse Code, Fortran, and Cobol), written languages, nursery rhymes, ancient alphabets, riddles, and military codes. Some semioticians pursue kinesics (the study of movement) to show that gestures—etiquette, liturgy, and pantomine, to name but a few—depend on cultural codes. Others examine food and culinary practices, color systems, the plot structures of myths, fairy tales, and detective stories, or even fortune-telling cards. Paralinguistic semioticians study the language of drums and whistles and such "vocal characterizers" as laughing, crying, whimpering, whispering, yawning, and belching. Indeed, in *The Name of the Rose*, when Eco's detective, Brother William of Baskerville, reminds his disciple and scribe, the novice Adso of Melk, to "recognize the evidence through which the world speaks to us like a great book," he is uttering the semiotician's credo. William, who is Umberto Eco's medieval *alter ego*, asserts that "the universe is . . . talkative . . . and it speaks not only of the ultimate things (which it does always in an obscure fashion) but also of closer things, and then it speaks quite clearly." Polyester or silk brocade, Coca-Cola or Château Haut-Brion are all signs in a complex system of signs called "culture." To quote Eco,

"People communicate with each other by various means, from the clothing they wear to the houses they live in."

That Eco should have chosen the Middle Ages as the setting for *The Name of the Rose* also seems appropriate, for there is perhaps no other period in European history as formless, indistinct, as resolutely indeterminate. It is a period of history defined not by itself but by its relationship to the two other periods—the classical age and the Renaissance—that surround it. The Renaissance humanists regarded the millennium that separated their age from the classical age as so different from both and as so characterless in itself that they called the period simply the *medium aevum*, "the Middle Ages," a term that has since been used by all historians.

In the Middle Ages, then, Eco has found yet another *opera aperta*, an historical "open work." For, like many an open work, the Middle Ages have no clear beginning. While some medievalists arbitrarily choose 410 A.D., the sack of Rome by Alaric, as the opening of the Middle Ages, and others delay the opening sixty-six years to 476 A.D., when Romulus Augustulus was deposed by Odoacer, most contend that the Roman Empire did not end in a cataclysmic "fall" but declined slowly and steadily from the third to the eighth century.

Neither do the Middle Ages have a definite end. Most historians feel that it is as indefensible to see a sudden end to medieval civilization as it is to see an abrupt beginning. They agree that the medieval world came to an end sometime during the fourteenth or fifteenth century, but then, depending on personal biases, they tend to connect it with a significant person or event—**William of Occam** or Giotto, the publication of Dante's *Divina commedia* or the nailing of Martin Luther's 95 theses on the door of the church at Wittenberg in 1517.

Like an open work, too, the Middle Ages have no well-defined personality. The interpretation of this period depends largely upon the historian's arrangement of the evidence. In the early Middle Ages (c. 400–1000), there seems to have been no solid structure on which to sustain a civilization. It was a period of extreme instability in which Europe was devastated by Vikings, Magyars, and Arabs and controlled at different times by Goths, Vandals, Burgundians, or Franks. The great cities of the Roman Empire were great no longer. There were dramatic shifts in the population. Intellectually, western Europe was cut off not only from the ancient culture but also from contemporary sources of learning and science, and most of its energy was spent in trying to preserve what was beautiful, good, and true in a declining culture that all too often seemed powerless before the invading barbarian hordes.

The high Middle Ages (1000–1300), on the other hand, seem to have been a period of growth and self-discovery. Europe revived, the economy recovered, and national dynasties and parliamentary institutions arose in England and France. The church was reformed and revitalized, as various churchmen attempted to define more clearly the church's spiritual powers and temporal prerogatives. An era of expansion and experimentation, it was still possible for a Benedictine monk like **Adelard of Bath** to forsake his cloistered life in order to travel extensively in the Near East collecting works of Greco-Arabic science (or for Eco's fictional novice, Adso, to roam among the cities of Tuscany, "partly out of idleness and partly out of a desire to learn"). It was during this time, too, that dialectic—the art of examining statements logically to determine their validity—flourished. Articles of faith became so subjected to logical analysis that wary clergymen like Peter Damian warned that theology was in danger of becoming the servant of philosophy.

It was a period of intellectual ferment in which new techniques of logical argument and a new rationalism were tried successfully, even if their proponents were sometimes assailed for their success. It was an age, too, when most controversies began and ended with **Aristotle.** During the thirteenth century, Western scholars managed to retrieve almost all of Aristotle's writings. Islamic Spain became the scholar's paradise—a Garden of Eden in which the Aristotelian corpus became the new Tree of the Knowledge of Good and Evil, and the serpent took the protean form of countless commentaries written on Aristotle works by Arab philosophers. The interpretation of Aristotle and his Moslem commentators led to new and often bitter rivalries between religious orders like the Franciscans and Dominicans.

The thirteenth century was also the age of the encyclopedia, of the great *summa* and the various *specula* ("mirrors"), which were intended to reflect and bring together in a single work all of human knowledge and divine truth. That century alone saw the publication of **Aquinas'** formidable *Summa Theologica* and *Summa contra Gentiles*, of **Bacon's** scientific encyclopedias—the *Opus maius* [Greater Work], *Opus minus* [Lesser Work], and *Opus tertium* [Third Work]—of **William of Occam's** *Summa logicae*, and of **Vincent of Beauvais'** monumental *Speculum maius* [Greater Mirror].

But before long, the high Middle Ages gave way to a period in which the intellectual openness of the preceding three centuries was tried and found guilty. During this period, social structures and philosophical assumptions were overthrown by climatic changes, famine, and a series of plagues, the most virulent of which was the Black Death of 1347–1350; political ideals and ethical standards were challenged by the Hundred Years' War between France and England and by the introduction into Europe of the weaponry of modern warfare—gunpowder and heavy artillery; and ecclesiastical institutions were threatened by the rise of nationalist feeling and by schism within the church. Western thought degenerated into pragmatic skepticism or mystic fideism, into flaccid subjectivity or stolid dogmatism. Aristotelianism was condemned in Paris—a disastrous turning point, according to several scholars, in the history not only of the Church but of Western thought. In the opinion of **Étienne Gilson,** the condemnation of Aristotle—a shameless display of force—was a sign of the Church's growing insecurity. In place of the painstaking refutation of error that one finds everywhere in the works of Thomas Aquinas, the Church simply "pronounced." There was no challenging of faulty logic by good logic, no mustering of sound arguments to overturn the unsound. Just a sim-

e *anathema sit*—one that would lead, on the one
famous curse upon "the whore, Reason," and,
the authoritarian reforms of the Council of
ı rent—in short, to the closing of the *opera aperta* that was the
Middle Ages.

In his book *Opera aperta*, Eco himself gives us yet another
reason for his fascination with the Middle Ages. For during this
period, there flowered a theory of allegory similar, in many ways,
to Eco's own semiotic theories. The Scriptures (and eventually
secular poetry as well) were believed to contain many meanings
and were able to be read immediately in four different ways:
literally, morally, allegorically, and anagogically. The medieval
reader, like Eco's semiotic reader of today, was acutely aware of
the fact that every passage, sentence, and trope was "open" to
a multiplicity of meanings which he had to discover. *Videmus
nunc per speculum et in aenigmate:* "for now we see through a glass,
darkly."

In *The Name of the Rose*, Eco also draws a parallel between
the nominalist controversies of the high Middle Ages and his
own semiotic theories. Indeed, the title of his novel—*The Name
of the Rose*—may be a sly allusion to the famous scholastic discussions of universals that arose in the wake of the revival of
Aristotelian logic. And the arguments that arose over universals—whether they are objects existing in their own right or only
"names," i.e. concepts that exist solely in the mind, whether
they are corporeal or incorporeal, whether they are separated
from sensible things or in sensible things—can be viewed as the
epistemological forerunners of today's investigations into the relationship between general semiotics and the philosophy of language.

Like the medieval monks he writes about, Eco's catholic
interests and rabid bibliomania are everywhere in evidence. *The
Name of the Rose* is brimming with esoterica on heresies, handi-
crafts, herbs, arcane codes, and quotations in classical and medieval Latin from the Apocalypse and the works of Virgil, Horace,

Isidore of Seville, Alain de Lille, and Bernard of Cluny, among others.

There are also playful allusions to such modern writers as James Joyce, Arthur Conan Doyle, and Jorge Luis Borges. Eco's sleuth—who has come as Louis IV's envoy to a Benedictine monastery in northern Italy to initiate negotiations between Pope John XXII and the dissident Franciscans but who discovers, shortly after his arrival, that he must first solve a series of grisly murders—is called Brother William of Baskerville. His name clearly identifies him as a medieval incarnation of Sherlock Holmes, one of whose most famous cases involved the mysterious hound responsible for the deaths of Sir Hugo, the master of the lonely, moor-encompassed Manor of Baskerville, and, it would seem, of Sir Hugo's descendant, Sir Charles Baskerville. William of Baskerville's disciple and scribe (and the book's narrator) is a Benedictine novice, Adso of Melk, whose name, especially in its French form (Adson), rhymes with "Watson." There are, moreover, other Holmesian elements—secret rooms and passages that bring to mind the adventures of the Speckled Band, Golden Pince-Nez, and Norwood Builder, and hidden manuscripts and secret codes that recall the adventures of the Second Stain and Dancing Men.

But perhaps no figure looms over *The Name of the Rose* more appealingly and ominously than that of Argentine writer Jorge Luis Borges, who has been metamorphosed into the character named Jorge of Burgos. Like Borges, Eco's monk Jorge is blind, "venerable in age and wisdom," and speaks Spanish as his native tongue. The narrator's ambivalent attitude toward the crafty old monk may be indicative of Eco's own literary love-hate relationship with Borges. The character Jorge is both a loving tribute and a tacit condemnation of Borges whose philosophy Eco no doubt considers not so much wrong-headed as wrong-hearted. In an interview with John Heilpern for *Vanity Fair* (June, 1984), Eco described himself as tragically optimistic: "I quote the definition of Emmanuel Mounier when he said his philosophy was an *optimisme tragique*. You know that life is tragic, but you have to look for any form of salvation. To be optimistically optimistic is stupid, I think. On the other hand, to be tragically pessimistic is neurotic. So tragically optimistic is the only way to deal with the world!''

Although Eco doubtless regards Jorge Luis Borges as a tragic pessimist, he shares with the Argentine writer a predilection for metaphysical arcana and a passionate conviction that the detective story is a useful metaphor for philosophy, art, history, and life itself. The mythic universes that Eco and Borges have created are filled, moreover, with some of the same symbols and images.

The labyrinthine library at the center of *The Name of the Rose* is an ingenious variation of Borges' "The Library of Babel," a nightmarish short story about man's inability to decipher a meaningless world. Not only is there a physical resemblance between Eco's library and Borges', which is "composed of an indefinite and perhaps infinite number of hexagonal galleries," "has a mirror in the hallway that duplicates all appearances," and represents the universe, but the narrator, an aging librarian, has spent his life in a futile search for one Book which possesses the secret of the world.

Labyrinths and mirrors are the two most common images in Borges' works. Labyrinths—symbols of a world too chaotic and illusory to be reduced to any human law—play a prominent role in Borges' "The Two Kings and their Two Labyrinths," in "The Garden of the Forking Paths," "The Waiting," "Ibn Hakkan al-Bokhari, Dead in His Labyrinth," and "The House of Asterion," to name a few. Mirrors, linked in Borges' writings to doubles and identity crises, unreality, art, and dreams, are used not only as motifs but as structuring devices as well. In *The Name of the Rose*, William of Baskerville, relying on the logic of Aristotle, the theology of Aquinas, and the cognitive empiricism of Roger Bacon, must decipher the riddle of the library with its distorting mirror before he is able to unravel the mystery of the monastery's murders.

Eco and Borges are likewise both fascinated with maps and compasses, manuscripts and books, emblematic for both of the world—the *liber mundi*—, fantastic alphabets and maddeningly undecipherable languages, which, for Borges, represent the mind of God whose reasons for creating man and the universe remain an unfathomable mystery.

Then there is the rose, variously symbolic of heavenly perfection and earthly passion, time and eternity, life and death. In medieval iconography, the rose is an emblem both of the passion of Christ and the purity of Mary. A symbol of completion, it is often depicted as the mystical center of the labyrinth. For Borges, the rose is symbolic not only of art and beauty but also of the vast gulf between language and the world. For example, in his haunting prose poem "A Yellow Rose," an Italian poet, Giambattista Marino, lies dying on a huge Spanish bed. As he gazes down at the yellow rose in a goblet in the garden beneath his balcony:

> the revelation occurred: Marino saw the rose as Adam might have seen it in Paradise, and he thought that the rose was to be found in its own eternity and not in his words; and that we may mention or allude to a thing, but not express it; and that the tall, proud volumes casting a golden shadow in a corner were not—as his vanity had dreamed—a mirror of the world, but rather one thing more added to the world.
>
> Marino achieved this illumination on the eve of his death, and Homer and Dante may have achieved it as well.

And, finally, there is Eco's enigmatic rose which, like the universal "rose" of the nominalists, can be predicated of many roses. To quote **Abelard,** "Once we allow the proposition, 'If there is a rose, there is a flower (*si est rosa, est flos*),' it is always true and necessary," even if the rose no longer exists or has never existed.

Eco's rose is the evanescent rose of Alain de Lille, which "blooms in the early morning" and then "flowers out, the flower deflowered" and of Bernard of Cluny's *De contemptu mundi: stat rosa pristina nomine, nomina nuda tenemus* ("Yesterday's rose endures in its name. We hold empty names"). For Bernard, the rose signifies the silent passing of the glories of the world, the brevity of human life, the decay of the body, the infinite sadness of mortality. For Adso at the end of *The Name of the Rose*, an old monk on the threshold of death, the rose is a nostalgic reminder of all "the wondrous and terrible events that he happened to observe in his youth." It is his mentor William of Baskerville, from whom he took his leave in Munich amid many tears; the momentary ecstasy of his "encounter with a maiden beautiful and terrible as an army arrayed for battle"; the first sight of an Italian abbey on a beautiful morning at the end of November. But it is also the scattered ruins of the Aedificium that he saw when he returned to revisit the abbey of his youth, the bookcases rotted by water and eaten by termites, the faded fragments of parchment, the ghosts of books. Then, too, Eco's many-petaled rose may signify the passing of the Middle Ages and the loss of a whole system of symbols, signs, dogmas, and rites within which the psychic life of Western man had been safely contained. *Stat rosa pristina nomine, nomina nuda tenemus*. Eco, the playful purveyor of the "open work," leaves it, finally, for his reader to decide.

1985

CHAPTER TWO

# A Brief Chronology
# of the Middle Ages

*This brief chronology includes the date of any event whose importance is central to an understanding of* The Name of the Rose.

| | |
|---|---|
| c. 480–547 | Saint Benedict of Nursia |
| 520 | Founding of the Benedictine order |
| c. 612 | Founding of the abbey of **Bobbio** |
| 872–882 | Papacy of John VIII |
| 909 | Founding of the abbey of Cluny |
| 999–1003 | Papacy of Sylvester II |
| 1079–1142 | **Peter Abelard** |
| c. 1171–1221 | Saint Dominic |
| 1179 | Lateran Council of 1179 |
| c. 1181–1226 | Saint Francis of Assisi |

| 1209 | Founding of the Franciscan order |
| c. 1214–c. 1292 | **Roger Bacon** |
| 1215 | Founding of the Dominican order (Order of Preachers) |
| 1224/25–1274 | **Saint Thomas Aquinas**, O.P. (Order of Preachers) |
| 1265 | Birth of Dante Alighieri of Florence |
| 1271–1276 | Papacy of Blessed Gregory X (Teobaldo or Tedaldo Visconti) |
| 1274 | **Second Council of Lyons** |
| 1277–1280 | Papacy of Nicholas III |
| 1279 | Papal bull *Exiit qui seminat*—most important interpretation of the Franciscan rule (See Eco 341.35/*411.23*) |
| c. 1285–c. 1349 | **William of Occam (Ockham)** |
| 1294 | Papacy of **Saint Celestine V** (Peter of Morrone) |
| 1294–1303 | Papacy of **Boniface VIII** (Benedict Gaetani) |
| 1301 | Teenaged Louis IV of Bavaria begins rule |
| 1303–1304 | Papacy of Blessed **Benedict XI** (Niccolo Boccasini) |

| | |
|---|---|
| 1305–1314 | Papacy of Clement V (Bertrand de Got) |
| 1307 | **Fra Dolcino** dies |
| 1309 | Papacy moves from Rome to Avignon, which becomes the center of western Christendom. The period known as the Babylonian Captivity begins. |
| 1311–1312 | Council of Vienne |
| 1312 | Papal bull *Exivi de Paradiso* (See Eco 53.17/*56.3–4*) |
| 1316–1334 | Papacy of **John XXII** (Jacques d'Euse of Cahors) |
| 1317 (April 13) | Papal bull *Quorundam exigit* (See Eco 338.36/*407.31*) |
| 1317 (December 30) | Papal bull *Sancta Romana* (See Eco 370.29/*447.9–10*) |
| 1321 | Death of Dante Alighieri of Florence |
| 1322 (May) | General chapter of Franciscans in Perugia |
| 1322 (December) | Papal bull *Ad conditorem canonum* (See Eco 55.38/*59.7–8* and 339.10/*408.10*) |
| 1323 | Canonization of **Saint Thomas Aquinas, O.P.** |
| 1323 (November 12) | Papal bull *Cum inter nonnullos* (See Eco 13.18/*6.2–3* and 339.18/*408.20*) |

| | |
|---|---|
| 1323 | **John XXII** asks Louis IV of Bavaria to abdicate |
| 1324 (May 22) | **Sachsenhausen Appellation** |
| 1324 (November 10) | Papal bull *Quia quorundam* (See Eco 338.36/*407.31*) |
| 1326 | Papal bull *Super illius specula* (See Eco 329.22/*397.17*) |
| 1327 (late November) | The setting of *The Name of the Rose* |
| 1328–1330 | Crowning of Louis IV as Holy Roman Emperor; Anti-papacy of Nicholas V (Pietro Rainalducci) |
| 1334 (December 4) | **John XXII** dies |
| 1347 (October 11) | Louis IV of Bavaria dies |
| 1362–1370 | Papacy of Blessed Urban V |
| 1367 | Papacy returns from Avignon to Rome—end of the so-called Babylonian Captivity |

# CHAPTER THREE

# An Annotated Guide to the Historical and Literary References in *The Name of the Rose*

*In this chapter the reader will find, in alphabetical order, biographical sketches of the important and not-so-important figures mentioned in* The Name of the Rose. *The section includes saints (as, for example, Agilulf and Aldemar, Angela of Foligno and Clare of Montefalco), heretics (from the Arnoldists, Beghards, and Bizochi to the Waldensians and Williamites), mythological allusions (Cockaigne and Cimmerian fog, Blemmyae and the bull of Phalaris) as well as the names and works of the most insignificant and obscure authors buried in the shelves of Eco's labyrinthine library.*

**Abelard, Peter** (1079–1142)    A French philosopher and theologian whose importance rests mainly on his ingenious solution to the problem of universals. Accepting Aristotle's definition of a universal as something that can be predicated of many things, Abelard maintained that universals are neither real things (since real things are individual) nor mere words (since universals signify a common reality that exists in things). Instead, he held that universals exist only in the mind but that they express the nature that individual things share in common.

Abelard is perhaps even more famous for his notorious love affair with Heloise, the niece of Fulbert, a canon of Notre Dame. Invited to live in Fulbert's house and supervise the education of the canon's young niece, Abelard fell in love with the lovely and learned teenager and made her pregnant. When their child was born, the unconventional couple named him Astrolabe. Then, to pacify Fulbert, Abelard agreed to marry Heloise secretly. Not long afterwards, however, to protect his reputation and further his career, Abelard convinced Heloise to enter a convent, which her uncle considered an evasion of responsibility. Fulbert took revenge by hiring men, who broke into Abelard's lodgings at night and castrated him.

After his downfall, which Abelard himself describes in his autobiography *Historia calamitatum* [*The Story of My Misfortunes*], he joined the Benedictines. The brilliant dialectician resumed his teaching career in Paris until 1121 when his treatise on the Blessed Trinity was condemned by the Council of Soissons.

Later, new charges of heresy were brought against Abelard by Bernard of Clairvaux which resulted in his condemnation by the Council of Sens. Abelard retracted some of his more controversial statements and died at a Cluniac priory in 1142. Two of Abelard's most important works were the *Dialectica*, on logic, and the *Sic et non* [Yes and No], an anthology of conflicting patristic texts.

**Abu-Bakr Muhammed ibn-Zakariyya ar-Razi** (c. 865–c. 925)    More commonly known to medieval Europe as Rhazes, he was a scientist, philosopher, and the greatest physician of the Muslim world. He held the post of physician-in-chief at the great hospital of Baghdad, where he authored many of his more than two hundred works on medicine. His greatest work, the *al-Hawi* or *Liber Continens*, was a monograph on smallpox and measles. He also wrote a famous treatise on stones in the kidneys and bladder. Rhazes believed in metempsychosis. His *Book of Secrets* was translated by Gerard of Cremona in the twelfth century. Like Eco's Jorge of Burgos, Rhazes was blind (or near-blind).

**Abul Asan al-Muchtar ibn-Botlan** (lived c. 1050)    Also

known as Ububchasym de Baldach, Ellucasim Elimittar, and
Albushasis. Albushasis was a Christian physician and theologian
of Baghdad. Besides teaching medicine and philosophy, he wrote
a number of works on a wide range of subjects. Albushasis wrote
a treatise on the Eucharist, one on simple remedies, especially
for the use of monks, a handbook on what to look for when
buying a slave (with a section on bodily defects.) He also wrote
*The Medical Dinner Party*, a clever skit on quacks, their ignorance
and arrogance, with remarks on the ethics of the medical profession. His major work was the *Takwim al-sihha* or *Theatrum
Sanitatis* [Theater of Health], a compendium of hygiene and
macrobiotics arranged in the form of tables—a method he borrowed from the astronomical writers.

**Adelard of Bath** (c. 1070–c. 1146)     An English philosopher,
scientist, and translator of works of Greco-Arabic science. Adelard
was a Benedictine who preferred travelling in the East to living
a cloistered life. Having mastered Arabic, he translated into Latin
an Arabic version of Euclid's *Elements* as well as an Arabic *Introduction to Astronomy*, the astronomical tables, and a ninth-century
*Introduction* by Mohammed ben Moses al Khwarizmi either to
astronomy or to the entire *quadrivium* (geometry, astronomy,
arithmetic, and music). He also wrote *Rules for the Abacus*, a work
on falconry, and a treatise on the astrolabe. His most important
work, which he wrote between 1111 and 1116, was the *Quaestiones
Naturales* [76 Questions on Nature] which owed a great deal to
Arabic learning.

**Adramelch, Alastor, and Azazel**     Adramelch (Adram-
melech) is a Babylonian god to whom the Sepharvites burned
their children as offerings (2 Kings 17:31). Alastor is an avenging
deity frequently invoked in Greek tragedy who pursues the guilty
and visits upon children the sins of their fathers. In Leviticus,
Azazel is the scapegoat. Elsewhere, Azazel is a fallen angel cast
out of Heaven either for tempting Adam or for refusing to worship him. He is a counterpart of Satan.

**Adso of Montier-en-Der**    A tenth-century Benedictine teacher and writer, he became abbot at Montier-en-Der c. 960 and, later, abbot of Saint-Bénigne at Dijon. Adso died at sea while travelling to the Holy Land and was buried in the Cycladic islands off Greece. A noted hagiographer, Adso wrote many lives of saints but is especially remembered for his apocalyptic letter to Queen Gerberga, *On the Origin and Time of the Antichrist*—the earliest extant version in the West of the legend of the Last World Emperor.

**Aelius Spartianus**    One of the six ostensible authors of the *Historia Augusta*, a collection of Latin biographies of Roman emperors, heirs to the throne, and pretenders from Hadrian (117–138) to Carinus and Numerianus (283–284). Many of the biographies are dedicated either to Diocletian (284–305) or Constantine the Great (306–337), and it was assumed that the work was written during their reigns. It is now accepted, however, that the dedications are fictitious and the *Historia Augusta* was composed later.

**Agilulf of Cologne, Saint** (died c. 750)    Much confusion surrounds Saint Agilulf and his cult. He seems to have been a Benedictine monk who later became bishop of Cologne. According to one account, he was martyred for discharging his episcopal duties too enthusiastically—a victim of the machinations of Charles Martel, Charlemagne's grandfather.

**Alanus de Insulis** (c. 1115–1202)    French theologian, preacher, and poet more commonly known as Alain de Lille. A Cistercian, Alain de Lille took part in the mystic reaction against scholasticism in the late twelfth century. Espousing an eclectic philosophy that combined scholastic rationalism and mysticism, Alain wrote a theological treatise, *The Art of the Catholic Faith*, in which he used mathematics to demonstrate the truth of the doctrines expressed in the creed. He also wrote *Contra Haereticos*, an attack on the Waldensians, Albigensians, Jews, and Saracens.

Among his many other works are two remarkable poems, the *Anticlaudianus*, an allegorical epic on the creation and perfection of the human soul that inspired Dante and Chaucer, and the *De Planctu Naturae* [Plaint of Nature], a delightful satire on human vices. In 1960, Alain's remains were exhumed and the well-preserved skeleton was that of a man in his late eighties or early nineties.

**Albertus Magnus, Saint** (1206–1280)   A Dominican teacher and scientist, Albertus Magnus (or Albert the Great) was educated at Padua and taught at Paris, where Thomas Aquinas was unquestionably his most brilliant student. He later taught at Cologne and was consecrated Bishop of Ratisbon (Regensburg). Well-versed in the works of Aristotle and of his Arab and Jewish commentators, he disseminated this knowledge throughout the Christian West. Against the Averroists, however, Albertus argued that each man had a separate active and passive intellect. Dante places him next to Thomas Aquinas in Paradise (*Paradiso* X).

**Albigensians**   See **Catharists.**

**Aldemar, Saint** (c. 950–?)   A Benedictine abbot and lover of animals. As a very young man, Aldemar became a monk at Monte Cassino. Once, when a swarm of bees had made a hive in one of the monastery's cupboards, Aldemar forbade the other monks to disturb them. After his death, his body was carried to Bocchignano in Abruzzi, where it remains today, and he is venerated as the town's patron saint.

**Aldhelm of Malmesbury** (c. 640–709)   Abbot, bishop, and perhaps the first important Anglo-Saxon writer. As abbot of Malmesbury, Aldhelm was responsible for the rebuilding of the church and monastery. Fond of the alliterative, tortuous, and obscure, he wrote *Carmina ecclesiastica* [Ecclesiastical Songs], a collection of religious poems, and *De laudibus virginum* [On the

Praises of Virgins], a lengthy didactic poem in hexameters. He also wrote an elaborate prose treatment of virginity, a treatise on grammar and metrics, and letters, including one on the date of Easter. Many of Aldhelm's Anglo-Saxon poems were sung to harp accompaniment in order to lure listeners to church.

**Alfred of Sareshel** (lived c. 1210) An English scientist and scholar, Alfred wrote glosses—comments and explanatory notes—on Aristotle's *De anima* [On the Soul] and *Parva Naturalia* [Short Works on the Natural Sciences] and translated the Pseudo-Aristotelian *De Vegetalibus*. His *Liber de congelatis* [Book on Hardened Substances] was a translation of the appendix to Avicenna's treatise on meteors. His revolutionary work *De Motu Cordis* [On the Movement of the Heart] was the first important study of the heart as principal organ of the soul and as seat of life. In it, Alfred cites the works of Aristotle and of other early physiologists such as Hippocrates, Galen, and Avicenna.

**Alhazen** (c. 965–1039) Ibn al-Haitham or Alhazen, the foremost Arab authority on optics, wrote an extraordinary treatise on the subject surpassing anything that has survived in Greek science. It was translated into Latin by the beginning of the thirteenth century. Unlike the Greek scientists Euclid and Ptolemy, who had assumed that light rays emanate from the eye, Alhazen proved that they travel to the eye from luminous objects. Alhazen discovered spherical aberration, produced his own plane and parabolic mirrors, and using the *camera obscura*, demonstrated that light and colors are not mixed in air.

**Alkindi** (born in the middle of the ninth century) Arab philosopher and scientist whose writings survive mostly in Latin translations. Alkindi applied the principles of Neo-Pythagorean mathematics not only to physics but to medicine as well. According to his theory of composite medicines, the effects of different medicines depend upon the geometrical proportions of the mixture of physical qualities such as warm, cold, dry, or moist. Alkindi was also interested in optics. He demonstrated that light travels in straight lines and treated such topics as optical illusions and the influence of mirrors, distances, and angle of vision on sight. In his treatise *De Radiis Stellatis* [On Stellar Rays], also called *The Theory of the Magic Art,* Alkindi affirms the astrological doctrine of radiation of occult influences from the stars. According to Alkindi, the variety and multiplicity of objects in nature depends upon two things: the diversity of matter and the varying influence of rays that flow from different stars. Each star has its own peculiar power and affects certain objects more than others. Alkindi also wrote a fascinating monograph on why the sky is blue.

**Al-Kuwarizmi** (c. 780–c. 850)     Perhaps the greatest name in early Arab mathematics and astronomy. Al-Kuwarizmi was familiar not only with Greek works on mathematics and astronomy but also with Indian systems. The Latin translations of his works introduced into European mathematics the Arabic or decimal system of numeration and also the term algebra, which first appears in a twelfth century translation of his *Book of Integration and Equation.* Extremely practical, Al-Kuwarizmi's *Algebra* is a collection of rules for the solution of linear and quadratic equations, elementary geometric propositions and more mundane inheritance problems involving the distribution of money. The word "algorism" is derived from Al-Kuwarizmi's name.

**Angela of Foligno, Saint** (c. 1248–1309)     Franciscan mystic. Angela of Foligno was a married woman who lived a relatively normal life until her late thirties when she experienced a singularly dramatic religious conversion. According to her own account, God summoned her to an austere life of chastity cloistered from the world. This life could not be embraced, however, as long as her husband and children were alive, and so the determined Angela prayed for their deaths. Her prayer was promptly answered, and before long devoted disciples gathered around her. Angela received divine revelations on the Trinity which were invariably followed by eight days of ecstatic trances during which she lay motionless and mute. She was persuaded by her Franciscan confessor to give an account of her intellectual illuminations and mystical graces. Her book, translated into Latin by her confessor and called *The Book of Visions and Instructions*, traces the twenty steps of penitence which carried Angela to the threshold of the mystical life.

**Angelus Clarenus** (died June, 1337)    Franciscan writer and translator. Shortly after joining the Franciscan order, Angelus Clarenus became involved with the Franciscan Spirituals. As a result, he was condemned to life imprisonment in 1275. Fourteen years later, he was freed by the minister general of the Franciscans, Raymond Gaufredi. Upon his release, Angelus sought and received from Pope Celestine V permission for himself and his followers to leave the Franciscan First Order and become Celestines—an authorization that was later voided by Celestine's successor, Boniface VIII. Angelus' attempts to obtain papal recognition for the Clareni (or Franciscan Celestines) from Pope Clement V (1305–1314) were futile, and under John XXII, he fared no better, largely because the new Franciscan minister general, Michael of Cesena, would not countenance a separate group within the order. Eventually, Angelus took the habit of the Benedictine Celestines (despite their opposition) and moved to Subiaco. Inquisitional proceedings were instituted against Angelus by John XXII in 1331, but the inquisitor mysteriously died. In addition to many controversial writings, Angelus translated from Greek the Rule of St. Basil and the *Scala* [Ladder] of John Climacus. In the early nineteenth century, the cause for Angelus' beatification was studied but promptly abandoned.

**Apollyon**    In Revelation 9:11, the angel of the bottomless pit. Apollyon is the Greek name of Abaddon ("the destroyer" in Hebrew), king of Hell. The name appears in Bunyan's *Pilgrim's Progress* and is often associated with witchcraft.

**Apuleius of Madaura** (c. 125–170 A.D.)    A Roman philosopher and prose writer born in Africa. Apuleius married a rich widow, Aemilia Pudentilla, whose relatives accused him of practicing magic to win her affection and brought a lawsuit against him; he was eventually acquitted. Apuleius' most famous work is the *Metamorphoses* [Transformations] or *The Golden Ass*, which is both a wonderful picaresque novel and a compelling spiritual autobiography. *The Golden Ass* is the story of Lucius of Thessaly, a young dabbler in magic who accidentally turns himself into an ass. After countless adventures, Lucius is finally restored to his human form by the Egyptian goddess Isis, whose priest he becomes. *The Golden Ass* resembles a short extant Greek work called *Lucius, or the Ass* by the Greek rhetorician and satirist Lucian of Samosata (c. 120–c. 180 A.D.). Lucian wrote parodies and satirical dialogues, the most famous of which are *Dialogues of the Gods*, *Dialogues of the Dead*, and *The True Story*.

**Aquinas, Saint Thomas** (1224/25–1274)    Dominican theologian and the greatest philosopher of the Middle Ages. The son of the count of Aquino, Thomas was educated at the Benedictine Abbey of Monte Cassino, at the University of Naples, where he was first attracted to the Dominicans, at Cologne, and at Paris. In 1244, he took the Dominican habit despite family opposition. On his way to Bologna, Thomas was kidnapped by his brothers and held prisoner in the family castle for over a year. Released, he continued his education as a Dominican and eventually lectured in Paris, Rome, Bologna, and Naples. Thomas Aquinas died on his way to the Council of Lyons (poisoned, according to Dante, who was following a popular but erroneous tradition in his *Purgatorio* XX).

The philosophy of Aquinas is essentially realist and concrete. There are no innate ideas. All knowledge is derived from sense experience. Corporeal objects act upon the sense organs. Through sensation we apprehend objects—but only particular objects. It then remains for the higher powers of the mind to act upon the sense data to form abstract and universal ideas.

Aquinas is perhaps best known for developing his five famous proofs of God's existence. According to the "Angelic Doctor," the existence of God is not self-evident but can be proved by human reason in five ways:

1. from motion (Following Aristotle, he argues that everything which is moved is moved by another—a thing cannot pass from potency to act except by something that is already in act. Since an infinite series of movers is impossible, we come in the end to an unmoved mover—God);
2. from cause and effect;
3. from the contingent and the necessary;
4. from the degrees of perfection found in things; and
5. from order or harmony in the universe.

Besides the august *Summa Theologica*, in which he attempts to reconcile Aristotelian philosophy with Christian theology, reason with faith, Aquinas wrote many other philosophical and theological works, including the *Summa contra Gentiles* and a commentary on the *Sentences* of Peter Lombard. Remarkable, also, was his ability to fuse seamlessly doctrine and verse in five majestic poems on the Eucharist.

**Areopagite, the**      See **Dionysius the Areopagite.**

**Arimaspi**      A mythical one-eyed tribe inhabiting Scythia who are continually at war with the griffins. The griffins are creatures, half eagle and half lion, large enough to carry off men in their claws. According to Pliny, the Arimaspi steal the gold that the griffins guard and make their drinking cups from the griffins' claws.

**Aristotle** (384–322 B.C.)      Greek philosopher and scientist. Born in Stagira in Thrace, Aristotle was one of Plato's students at the Academy in Athens. After Plato's death in 347, Aristotle settled in Assos, near Troy, where there were excellent facilities for research in marine biology. Later, he became tutor to Alexander the Great at the Macedonian court in Pella and taught the young prince, among other things, political philosophy, the natural sciences, and Homer. In 335, Aristotle returned to Athens and set up in the intellectual capital of the world a school and a kind of research foundation called the Lyceum. There was a library, museum, and map collection. The Lyceum attracted students from different parts of the Greek world who were eager to work on projects directed by the great Aristotle himself.

Perhaps Aristotle's most important contribution to Western thought is the *Organon* [The Instrument], his monumental treatise (actually, a collection of treatises) on deductive and inductive logic, which dominated the later Middle Ages. In it, Aristotle asserted that any logical argument could be reduced to a sequence of three propositions (two premises and a conclusion) called a syllogism, and that three laws—the law of identity (A is A), the law of contradiction (A cannot be both A and not A), and the law of the excluded middle (A must be either A or not A)— were basic to all logical thought. Aristotle's systematic study of valid inference so shaped the thinking of Western man that, until the ascendancy of symbolic logic in the nineteenth century, which replaced language with mathematical concepts, the terms "logic" and "Aristotelian logic" were largely synonymous.

Among Aristotle's other major works are the *Physics* and the *Metaphysics*, in which he deals with problems of the biological and natural sciences such as matter, movement, time, and space, enumerates the four causes of physical change—material, formal, efficient, and final—and then ends with a discussion of God; the *Rhetoric*, a study of the art of persuasion; the *Poetics*, Aristotle's analysis of tragedy and epic, a classic that has influenced Italian, French, and English literature and dramatic criticism from the sixteenth century onward; the *Politics*, the last significant work of Greek political thought; the *Nicomachean Ethics*, ten books on ethics, happiness, and the good; the *De Anima* [On the Soul], the first important work in the field of psychology—a treatment of sensation, thought, imagination, and reason; and several biological works, such as the *Historia animalium* (on the classification and characteristics of animals), the *De partibus animalium* [On the Parts of Animals], and *De generatione animalium* [On the Generation of Animals].

Over the centuries, the writings of Greek, Latin, and Arab commentators less gifted and more dogmatic than Aristotle transformed his thought into the rigid, authoritarian system that often tyrannized the later Middle Ages. Indeed, Thomas Aquinas' brilliant synthesis of Christian doctrine and Aristotelian method was regarded by many as the ultimate philosophy.

**Armageddon**     The name given in the Book of Revelation to the battlefield where the forces of good and evil will meet on the "day of God Almighty," Judgment Day, in the last great struggle for supremacy. The name may be derived from Har ("hill" in Hebrew) and Megiddo, a fortified hill town overlooking the plain of Esdraelon in Galilee in north central Palestine, where many battles were fought in the early history of the Israelites.

**Arnaldus Amalrici** (1160–1225)     Cistercian abbot, archbishop of Narbonne, and papal legate of Pope Innocent III. In 1201, Arnaldus (also called Arnaud Amaury) became abbot general of the Cistercian order. Eight years later, armed with a papal commission, Arnaldus organized a crusade against the Albigensians. After raising an army at Lyons in June 1209, he and his followers stormed and captured Béziers on July 22. It was there, in the midst of one of history's bloodiest massacres, that Arnaldus is reputed to have made his infamous remark, "Kill them all. God knows his children."

**Arnold of Brescia** (c. 1100–1155)     A student of Peter Abelard in Paris, Arnold joined the Canons Regular of St. Augustine and became prior of their monastery in Brescia. He was a radical reformer who proposed the Church's total abandonment of riches and temporal power. In 1139, the Second

Lateran Council condemned Arnold's statements and forced him to leave Italy. Later, Bernard of Clairvaux was instrumental in having Arnold banished from France. Eventually, Arnold was captured by the Emperor Frederick I Barbarossa and hanged in Rome. His body was burned and his ashes were scattered over the Tiber. Arnold's followers, the Arnoldists, regrouped after Arnold's death and became more fanatical. They rejected completely the power of the hierarchy and declared invalid any sacrament administered by a cleric who owned worldly possessions. In 1184, the Council of Verona condemned the Arnoldists as heretics.

**Arnoldists**     See **Arnold of Brescia.**

**Artemidorus** (Second century A.D.)     Greek dream interpreter from Daldis (in modern Turkey). He wrote the earliest extant Greek treatise on the interpretation of dreams, the *Oneirocritica*, in five books, whose most outstanding characteristic is its rational, practical approach.

**Astomats**     A people of India who are said to have no mouths. They are mentioned by Pliny the Elder in his *Natural History*.

**Ausonius** (died c. 395 A.D.)     A Christian Latin poet and teacher, Ausonius was born in Bordeaux and educated there and at Toulouse. Perhaps his most memorable work is the *Mosella*, a delightful poem about the river Moselle, describing in detail the fish found in it, the buildings on its banks, the vines in the adjacent country. This guidebook in verse, marked by a true love of nature, is sometimes called the first poem in French literature. Ausonius also wrote the *Parentalia*, thirty short poems lavishly praising deceased friends and relatives, and a collection of letters to his friend and pupil Paulinus of Nola, which gives us a fascinating glimpse into the conflict between Christian and pagan values in the fourth century A.D.

**Averroes** (1126–1198)    Arab philosopher. Averroes was born in Cordoba of an aristocratic Spanish Arab family. Besides his philosophical works, he wrote a digest of Islamic law and a compendium of medicine which was used in Europe for centuries. Averroes began his philosophical career by publishing summaries of the works of Aristotle as well as commentaries on the Arabic translations of Aristotle. He also wrote an apologia in which he argued the right of Muslim scholars to pursue philosophy, a treatise on Islamic theology, and a detailed rebuttal of al-Ghazzali's attack on the philosophers which led to his trial in 1195 as a heretic by the conservative religious community of Cordoba, his condemnation, and exile. Averroes was reprieved shortly before his death in 1198.

Averroes' philosophy is essentially Aristotelian. Forms and matter (and thus the world) are eternal. The existence of God is proved by the need for a First Mover and by the signs of providence in the world. God's activity consists not in creating the world from nothing, but in giving form to a matter that would otherwise be mere potentiality.

Averroes saw no conflict between philosophy and Islam. According to Averroes, the Koran expresses the truth for all men imaginatively, sometimes even in symbolic language, whereas philosophy expresses it in scientific prose for the limited use of scholars.

**Avicenna** (980–1037)    Arab philosopher, scientist, and medical writer. Born near Bukhara, Avicenna was a brilliant student. By the time he was a teenager, he had already earned a reputation as a distinguished physician. Once, Avicenna had to flee Khwarizm to elude a sultan who was determined to add him to the collection of notables detained in his palace. After a nomadic existence, Avicenna died at Hamadan, leaving behind a great number of writings.

Avicenna's philosophy was a mixture of Aristotelianism and Neo-Platonism. His *Kitab al-Shifa* [Book of Healing] was a comprehensive account of all knowledge with sections on logic (including rhetoric and poetics), physics (including psychology and natural history), mathematics, and metaphysics. Avicenna is especially important for his contributions to the field of medicine. His *Qanun* [Canon] is a voluminous work on medicine and pharmacology, which remained the standard textbook in Europe until the late seventeenth century. Much of Avicenna's scientific and medical information was written in unpolished verse, presumably as a memory device rather than a naive attempt at literary composition.

Despite his passion for philosophy, Avicenna was a devout Muslim and wrote several theological works. Some of his later writings display a mystical tendency and the influence of Gnosticism. These works, often allegorical in content, played a significant role in the evolution of Sufism.

**Ayyub al-Ruhawi** (c. 760–835)   Syrian writer and translator. Also known as Job of Edessa, Ayyub al-Ruhawi was a member of the court of caliph al-Mamun of Baghdad, who gathered around himself a number of Syrian translators and scribes who translated into Arabic the Greek, Syrian, and Persian texts which the Arabs had found in conquered Persia. Ayyub al-Ruhawi, a Nestorian, was a prolific writer, but only two of his works are extant—his treatise on canine hydrophobia and a compendium of philosophy and the natural sciences in Syriac entitled *The Book of Treasures*.

**Bacon, Roger** (c. 1214–c. 1292)   Franciscan scholar and scientist. Born in England, Roger Bacon attended Oxford. While lecturing at Paris on Aristotelian and pseudo-Aristotelian works, Bacon met Pierre of Maricourt, who wrote on the magnet and astrolabe, and became acquainted with the pseudo-Aristotelian *Secretum Secretorum* [Secret of Secrets]. These two events seem to have been instrumental in turning Bacon's attention to the experimental sciences and languages. In 1257, Bacon joined the Franciscans, but his relations with the order seem to have been poor from the start. Even though he was allowed to carry out experiments on the nature of light and on natural phenomena such as the rainbow, he was actually imprisoned for a time by the order for "teaching novelties."

Bacon produced scientific encyclopedias such as the *Opus maius* [Greater Work], *Opus minus* [Lesser Work], and *Opus tertium* [Third Work]. Convinced that too much importance was being attached to the role of logic in confirming or refuting speculative hypotheses, Bacon relied more and more on mathematical demonstration and experimental investigation. Much of Bacon's best work was done in the field of optics. And although he has been variously credited with the discovery of eyeglasses, the telescope, and gunpowder, he himself never claims to have invented them. His reputation as a magician came after his death.

**Baylek al-Qabayaki** (c. 1215–c. 1285)    Muslim mineralogist who lived in Cairo from c. 1242 to c. 1282. In 1282/83, he wrote a work entitled *The Treasure of Merchants Concerning the Knowledge of Precious Stones*. It has a section on the floating compass and its use by mariners, which he himself had observed in the Mediterranean.

**Beatus of Liebana** (died February 19, 798)    Abbot and writer born near Santander in Spain. Beatus wrote a popular if uninspired commentary on the Apocalypse in twelve books. More important than the text, however, are the illustrations and illuminations of many Beatus manuscripts, which clearly show the influence of Celtic, Coptic, and Mozarabic styles on Spanish art. These illustrations are believed to have inspired the Romanesque sculptors at Moissac in southern France, since the tympanum there has twenty-four Ancients holding, as viols, Spanish guitars that are strikingly similar to those found in a Beatus manuscript of the same scene.

**Bede, Saint** (673–735)    English monk, historian, and scholar. Known also as "the Venerable Bede," he lived and died in the twin monasteries of Wearmouth and Jarrow in Northumbria. Bede was only seven years old when he entered the monastic school of Wearmouth-Jarrow. Under the supervision of Benedict Biscop, one of England's greatest scholars, and Ceolfrith, Bede learned Latin, Greek, and Hebrew. He composed poems in English, only one of which, the *Death Song*, survives. His most important Latin poem describes, in about one thousand dactylic hexameters, the life and miracles of Cuthbert of Lindisfarne. Bede's most outstanding work is his *Historia ecclesiastica gentis Anglorum* [Ecclesiastical History of the English People], which he completed around 731. Filled with wonderful stories, such as Caedmon and his poetic gift, Gregory the Great and the English slaves, and the martyrdom of Saint Alban, Bede's remarkable history is, even today, our most dependable source for much of Anglo-Saxon history. Bede also wrote grammatical treatises, popular ecclesiastical biographies, such as the *Martyrology*, commentaries on the Scriptures, and a compendium of the physical sciences entitled *De natura rerum* [On the Nature of Things]. The title of Venerable was bestowed on him shortly after his death.

**Beghards**    A fraternity of laymen that originated in the thirteenth century in Flanders. This movement was the male counterpart of the Beguines, a sisterhood that arose in the twelfth century in the Netherlands. Beghards and Beguines professed no vows. While they remained in their communities, however, they promised to observe religious chastity, but they could leave to marry whenever they desired. Both groups stressed the importance of prayer and good works. The Beguines frequently engaged in teaching, nursing, and lace-making, while the Beghards were fullers, dyers, and weavers. Suspected of heretical tendencies, they were often confused with the Fraticelli, Franciscan Spirituals, the Apostolici, and the Brothers and Sisters of the Free Spirit. They were suppressed by the Council of Vienne in 1312.

**Benedict XI, Blessed** (1240–1304)      Pope from 1303 to 1304. Born Niccolo Boccasini, he entered the Dominicans in 1254 and later became master general of the order. He was an eminent scholar and wrote commentaries on the Psalms, Job, Matthew, and the Apocalypse. He was also a great peacemaker. Benedict managed to keep the Dominicans loyal to Pope Boniface VIII and later softened Boniface's *Clericis laicos* to heal the breach between King Philip IV of France and the papacy. He died suddenly in 1304, poisoned, many believed, by Guillaume de Nogaret whom he had excommunicated.

**Bernard of Clairvaux, Saint** (1090–1153)      Abbot, theologian, and Doctor of the Church. After several years of riotous living, Bernard decided to join the Cistercians, where he observed the strictest rule of the time with such singular devotion that after only three years he was chosen to found a new abbey, Clairvaux ("Clear Valley"), in France. Despite his poor health, Bernard never lost an opportunity to denounce the powerful Benedictine abbey of Cluny, whose ostentation and relaxed interpretation of the Rule of St. Benedict he considered shamefully decadent. In 1140, convinced that the teaching of Abelard posed a serious threat to the Christian faith, Bernard was instrumental in bringing about his condemnation. In 1146 or 1147, he preached the Second Crusade, which eventually ended in failure. Finally, in 1153, Bernard died, consumed by years of fanatical asceticism. He was canonized by Pope Alexander III in 1174.

Bernard wrote more than three hundred sermons, the most inspired of which were preached on the Song of Songs. He was an enthusiastic Mariologist, describing in detail the role and importance of Mary, the mother of Jesus, in Christian doctrine and especially in the work of the Redemption.

**Bernard of Cluny** (c. 1100–1156)      Benedictine monk and poet. Sometimes called Bernard of Morlaix, he is best known for his *De contemptu mundi* [On Contempt of the World], a long satirical poem of about 3000 lines in Latin, which he wrote c.

1140. The poem is a biting denunciation of the wickedness of his time, a savage indictment of a world edging toward destruction. Written in dactylic hexameter, it spares neither clergy nor laity—not even the Roman curia itself. The spectacular descriptions of heaven and hell have often been likened to Dante's, and the entire work ends on an apocalyptic note. Eco has borrowed from Bernard's poem *"Est ubi gloria nunc Babyloniae?"* ("Where is the glory of Babylon now?") and the delectably plaintive line *Stat rosa pristina nomine, nomina nuda tenemus.*

**Bizochi**     One of the heretical sects mentioned in the bull *Sancta Romana* (1317) by Pope John XXII, who does not distinguish them from the Fraticelli, Brothers of the Poor Life, or the "Beghini."

**Blemmyae**     A fabled people living in Africa who have no heads. Pliny the Elder says that their eyes and mouths are on their chests and they feed on human flesh.

**Bobbio**     A Benedictine abbey in northern Italy founded by Irish monks under the leadership of Saint Columban c. 612. Bobbio was one of the greatest centers of medieval learning and was especially famous for its impressive library.

**Boethius** (c. 480–524)     Roman philosopher and Christian theologian. Born in Rome, Boethius was probably the last important Roman writer to understand Greek. He has been called "the last great classical scholar of antiquity" and "the first of the medieval scholastics." His writings reflect both heritages—classical and Christian—and many of his works seem motivated by a desire either to preserve classical knowledge or to defend Christianity. Accused of conspiracy against the Emperor Theodoric the Ostrogoth and of sacrilege for practicing mathematics and astrology, Boethius was imprisoned and executed. Shortly before his death, in prison, Boethius wrote his most original work, *The Consolation of Philosophy*, an allegory in five books, in which

Philosophy in the form of a beautiful woman comes to him as a comforter and explains that man's unhappiness is primarily the result of his inability to understand his own nature and fate. The work, deeply personal if pagan in spirit, is reminiscent of Apuleius' *Golden Ass* and Augustine's *Confessions*. King Alfred the Great, Chaucer, and Queen Elizabeth I all did translations of *The Consolation of Philosophy*. Boethius himself translated Aristotle and wrote a treatise on the Trinity (for which Aquinas later wrote a commentary) as well as manuals on logic, arithmetic, and music.

**Bogomils**     Members of a neo-Manichaean religious movement that flourished in the Balkans between the ninth and fifteenth centuries. Probably founded by a priest named Bogomil, the sect originated in Bulgaria as a reaction against the pomp of Byzantine life. The sect's adherents were opposed to the ruling classes and to church hierarchy, specifically that of the recently established Bulgarian Orthodox Church, which they hoped to reform in the name of evangelical Christianity. The central teaching of Bogomilism was that the visible material world is the creation of the devil and is totally evil. Thus they rejected the doctrine of the Incarnation, Baptism, the Eucharist, and the cross and condemned marriage, the priesthood, church buildings, the eating of meat, and the drinking of alcohol, among other things. In the twelfth century, certain Bogomils established relations with the antiauthoritarian Catharists and Albigensians of northern Italy and southern France and influenced their doctrines and rituals.

**Bonagratia of Bergamo**     See **Michael of Cesena.**

**Bonaventure of Bagnoregio, Saint** (c. 1217–1274)     Italian cardinal, philosopher, theologian, and Doctor of the Church. After joining the Franciscans in 1243/44, Bonaventure taught at the University of Paris until he was elected minister general of the order. As general, he interpreted the mission of the newly established order of Saint Francis (Order of Friars Minor) and gave it direction. In 1274 he was created cardinal bishop of Albano by Pope Gregory X, whose election to the papacy he had supported. Later that year, he was a key figure at the Second Council of Lyons, where he died unexpectedly during one of the council sessions. Among his major works, Bonaventure wrote a commentary on the *Sentences* of Peter Lombard and a defense of mendicant orders entitled *The Apology of the Poor*. Bonaventure maintained that the world is a reflection of God and that man is able to know God through the mirror of created nature. Dante perspicaciously placed Bonaventure among the saints in his *Paradiso*. It was not until 1482, however, that he was officially declared a saint.

**Boniface VIII** (c. 1235–1303)    Pope from 1294 to 1303. Boniface's pontificate is remembered especially for the bitter struggle of Church and State that erupted between the papacy and the French monarch Philip IV of France. Shrewd, ambitious, autocratic, and irascible, Boniface VIII, then Benedict Gaetani, was instrumental in persuading his saintly but incompetent predecessor Celestine V to abdicate. But unable to appreciate that a new era of limited papal power was dawning, Boniface committed the papacy to lavish and imprudent claims in the temporal sphere. In his bull *Clericis laicos* (1296), he declared that any ruler who taxed his clergy without prior papal approval would incur automatic excommunication. Later, in his bull *Unam Sanctam* (1302), perhaps the most important medieval document on spiritual and temporal power, he proclaimed the right of popes to institute and judge kings. In 1303, the papal palace was seized by Philip's forces; Boniface collapsed, and died three weeks later.

**Brothers (and Sisters) of the Free Spirit**    A name applied to members of different sects from the twelfth to fifteenth centuries who shared a belief in the "Free Spirit"—that is, in a wholly free intellect incapable of any wrong and containing within itself the spark of an all-pervasive godhead. Idealistic pantheists, they argued that all creatures are identical with the Creator, man can become God, man is incapable of sin, and there is no resurrection from the dead.

**Buridan, John** (c. 1290–c. 1360)     French philosopher. Very little is known about John Buridan. Except for one visit to the Papal Curia at Avignon, his entire life was spent at the University of Paris, where he was an important figure in the Nominalist debates. Buridan wrote innumerable commentaries on Aristotle and Porphyry. Because of his theories on the nature of weight and the acceleration of falling objects, he is also considered the precursor of the great Renaissance scientists Copernicus and Galileo. But Buridan is perhaps most famous for an ass. "Buridan's ass" is a philosophical fable illustrating the doctrine of free will. An ass, left midway between two bales of hay, cannot choose one of them and dies of hunger. The fable asserts that a man in the same situation would use his free will to resolve the dilemma. While this fable is commonly attibuted to Buridan, the example that he actually gives in his commentary on Aristotle's *De caelo* is of a dog.

**Catharists**     Adherents of a heretical sect that flourished in Europe from the eleventh to thirteenth century. The Catharist philosophy originated in dualism, a system that assumes the existence of two eternal principles, Good (spirit) and Evil (matter) and demands a life of austere self-discipline aimed at freeing the good spirit from the evil prison of the body. The Manichaeans were among the earliest dualists. Similarly, the Paulicians of Armenia and the Bogomils of Bulgaria held dualistic beliefs.

The Catharists were especially powerful in northern Italy and in southern France, where they were called Albigensians. Many Catharists received the "Consolamentum," an imposition of hands that bestowed the spirit. They were consequently invited to live communal lives of perpetual poverty, chastity, and asceticism. The elect who fell short of the rigid obligations of the Consolamentum were subjected to a dramatic "reconsolation of the soul"—a forced death by starvation or asphyxiation. Eventually the Catharists became fragmented and disappeared.

**Celestine V, Saint** (1215–1296)    Pope from July 5 to December 13, 1294. Born Peter of Murrone, he joined the Benedictine order but lived most of his life as an itinerant preacher or as a hermit on various mountains, including Monte Murrone (Morrone), where he helped to found the Celestines. After the death of Pope Nicholas IV in 1292, the intense rivalry between the Orsini and Colonna factions made the election of a new pope virtually impossible. Finally, after more than two years, the conclave elected the unworldly Peter of Murrone. Realizing his administrative incompetence, Celestine issued a bull declaring a pope's right to abdicate and on December 13 promptly resigned.

**Celestinians**    A branch of the Benedictine order, also called Hermits of Saint Damian or Hermits of Morrone (Murrone). They were founded in 1264 by Peter of Murrone, who, thirty years later, became Pope Celestine V. The Hermits were especially renowned for their perpetual abstinence from meat and the austerity of their way of life. The name Celestinians was also given to some Franciscan Spirituals when Celestine V took them under his special protection. They were distinct from the Benedictine Celestinians.

**Cimmerian fog**    In the eleventh book of the *Odyssey*, Homer says that the Cimmerians lived beyond the Ocean "hidden in fog and cloud" and that "the radiant sun never shines down upon them with its rays . . . a ruinous night is always spread over these wretched mortals." The Greek historian Herodotus later identified the Cimmerians with the early inhabitants of Russia.

**Circumcellions**    A band of rustic fanatics during the fourth and fifth centuries A.D. who joined the ranks of the **Donatists**. They called themselves the "soldiers of Christ" but were, in fact, terrorists. Originally, they used only cudgels, which they called "Israelites," to batter their victims, on the ground that Saint Peter had been commanded by Jesus to put away his sword when the high priests came to arrest him. But later the Circumcellions employed swords as well. Their rabid desire for martyrdom often led them to commit suicide, especially by flinging themselves from cliffs, jumping into fires, threatening to murder passers-by who refused to kill them, or, by their violent crimes, forcing magistrates to execute them. Although the Donatists seem to have been acutely embarrassed by their deranged supporters, they still buried these suicides.

**Cistercians**     A monastic order founded in 1098 and named after the original community established at Cîteaux in Burgundy. The founders, led by Saint Robert de Molesme, were a group of Benedictine monks from the abbey of Molesme who were unhappy with its loose observance of the Rule of Saint Benedict. Seeking to live a solitary life dedicated to the strictest interpretation of the Benedictine rule, they demanded long fasts and little sleep, reintroduced manual labor for monks, simplified the liturgy, and banned golden ornaments and rich vestments. The Cistercian order was less interested in learning than in prayer, so their libraries were never impressive. By the time Saint Bernard of Clairvaux died, the total number of Cistercian abbeys was 338.

**Clare of Montefalco, Saint** (c. 1275–1308)     Augustinian mystic. For a while Clare observed the Franciscan rule, but in 1290 she became a member of her sister Joan's Augustinian convent at Montefalco. The next year she was elected abbess against her will. Clare's life was one of extreme austerity: as penance for a violation of silence, she would stand barefoot in snow while she recited the Lord's Prayer a hundred times. Her meditation, especially when centered on Christ's Passion, carried her to a trancelike state of ecstasy. She was also said to have possessed the gift of miracles. Clare's body is preserved intact, its dissected heart purportedly revealing in some fibrous tissue formations similar to the cross and other instruments of the Passion. Clare of Montefalco was canonized in 1881.

**Clement of Alexandria** (c. 150–c. 215 A.D.) A Greek Christian writer and Father of the Church. The son of educated parents, Clement was born either in Athens or Alexandria. After his conversion to Christianity, he succeeded his teacher Pantaenus as head of the Catechetical School of Alexandria. He wrote an *Exhortation to the Greeks* to convert his readers, Alexandria's pagan intellectuals, to Christianity. He also wrote the *Stromata* ("Miscellanies" or "Carpet Bags"), a collection of ancient wisdom in eight books, to demonstrate to his catechumens the superiority of Christianity to secular learning, particularly to Greek philosophy.

**Cluniac order** The Benedictines.

**Cluny** A Benedictine abbey that was one of the most important and powerful centers of Christianity in the Middle Ages. Founded in 909, it is located in the Rhone Valley.

**Cockaigne** A mythic land of luxury and idleness famed for its exquisite food. Candies grow like flowers at the edge of forests, perfumed wine springs up from fountains, roasted pigeons soar through the air, and cakes fall like rain from the sky. The Royal Palace of Cockaigne is made out of icing; the houses, of barley sugar. Its streets are paved with pastry. The people of Cockaigne, moreover, enjoy a kind of immortality. When they reach the age of fifty, they become ten-year-olds again. The name "Cockaigne" probably means "the land of cakes."

**Coena Cypriani** Written for the amusement of Pope John VIII by John the Deacon, the *Coena Cypriani* is a ninth-century narrative about the marriage feast of King Johel at Cana in Galilee to which countless persons from the Old and New Testaments are invited. In staccato fashion, the wedding guests are introduced with some of the distinctive traits or idiosyncrasies they possess in the Bible. The work, an interminable catalogue of biblical characters relieved occasionally by a crude joke or obscene remark, ends with the guests returning home.

**Cynocephali** ("dog-headed")    Either African apes with dogs' heads (according to Pliny the Elder) or a race of savages (according to Isidore of Seville).

**Dionysius the Areopagite** (Sixth century A.D.)    Also called Pseudo-Dionysius, Dionysius the Areopagite is the *nom de plume* of the author of four relatively obscure sixth-century works in Greek on liturgical and mystical theology. By publishing his writings as the work of the Dionysius who was converted to Christianity after hearing a sermon St. Paul delivered on the Areopagus of Athens (Acts 17:34), the author no doubt hoped his works would gain in stature and authority. The four works, Neoplatonist in their orientation, deal with the heavenly hierarchy, the ecclesiastical hierarchy, the divine names and mystical theology. Dionysius' hierarchies of heaven and earth are described as triads, proceeding from the Trinity and descending in threes through the nine choirs of angels to the earthly church of bishops, priests, and deacons. *The Divine Names* is his classic on man's knowledge of God from the Scriptures. Using the Neoplatonic thought of Proclus to interpret theology, Dionysius gives an account of the various names that can be applied to God as, for example, the Good, Unity, Trinity, Love, Beauty, Being, Wisdom, Reason, etc.

**Dolcino of Novara, Fra** (died 1307)    Leader of the heretical Apostolici. Raised and educated by a priest from Vercelli, Dolcino ran away in 1291 to become a member of the sect of Apostolici or Pseudo-Apostles founded by Gherardo Segarelli. When Segarelli was executed in 1300, Dolcino became the sect's new leader. Before long, nearly four thousand disciples had gathered at Novara around Dolcino, won over by his personal charm, persuasive discourse, and effortless ability to interpret Scripture. The Apostolici practised absolute poverty but pillaged to survive. To put an end to their activities, Pope Clement V agreed to help the citizens of Novara. Dolcino was finally taken prisoner on March 23, 1307. He was executed; his body was cut into pieces and burned.

The Apostolici obeyed God alone; they rejected completely the authority of the Church because of the depravity of its clergy. Dolcino, a millennialist, prophesied the coming of a supreme pontiff appointed by God himself after the apocalyptic destruction of the existing church with its corrupt hierarchy. The new church, committed to virtue and evangelical poverty, would be governed by Dolcino's disciples.

**Donatists**    Members of a fourth and fifth century Christian schismatic sect in North Africa, who asserted that the validity of a sacrament depended on the worthiness of the person who administered it. The movement derived its name from Donatus, the leader of this radical group of dissident clergymen. When the emperor Constantine refused the Donatists a share in the benefactions he had given to the clergy and congregations of north Africa, they appealed to him. Three times, the emperor and his tribunals decided against the Donatists, which led to their questioning the right of the emperor to interfere in the church. Constantine responded by ordering the military suppression of the Donatists and the confiscation of their property. In 321, when he realized that these repressive measures only exacerbated their fanaticism, Constantine adopted a more tolerant attitude, leaving the Donatists "to the judgment of God." Donatism finally disappeared in the seventh century when the Muslims conquered Africa.

**Eckhart, Johannes** (c. 1260–1328)    German Dominican theologian and mystic philosopher, also known as Meister Eckhart. Eckhart joined the Dominican order and was eventually elected provincial of the Dominican province of Saxony. He was a prolific writer in both German and Latin who ran into difficulties with ecclesiastical authorities in 1326. One hundred propositions drawn from his sermons were declared heretical. To defend himself before a papal commission, Eckhart went to Avignon, but before his case was concluded, he died. Influenced as much by Neoplatonism as by Thomas Aquinas, Eckhart argued the absolute transcendence and unknowability of God. He also held that nothing has real existence but God. Creatures have no being or existence in themselves. The existence of God's creatures is the existence of God Himself, who enjoys with His creatures the closest of all relationships. To many, Eckhart's mystical statements seemed pantheistic and hence heretical, though he always showed that they were capable of being explained in an orthodox sense.

**Floro (Florus)** (lived c. 140 A.D.)     Roman poet and historian. Florus was a close friend of the emperor Hadrian, who traded witticisms with him. Besides a number of pleasant poems in different meters, Florus wrote an academic *Dialogue* on whether Virgil is more of an orator than poet and an *Epitome of the Wars of the Roman People* in two books, which is occasionally interesting but more often bombastic and inaccurate.

**Fraticelli**     A term of contempt for heretical Franciscans, "Fraticelli" means "little friars." The Fraticelli can be further divided into the Fraticelli de Paupere Vita, who were the successors of the Franciscan Spirituals under the leadership of Angelus Clarenus, and the Fraticelli de Opinione, who were the followers of Michael of Cesena.

**Fronto, Marcus Cornelius** (c. 100–c. 166 A.D.)     Roman orator and philologist. Educated at Carthage and Alexandria, Fronto gained a reputation as a successful lawyer in Hadrian's time. Later he was made tutor to the future emperor Marcus Aurelius, who, when Fronto died, placed his statue in the Senate and included his bust among his own household gods. A champion of archaism, Fronto was the most brilliant orator of his day. Many of his letters survive, some of which are covering letters to artificial exercises in rhetoric such as *In Praise of Smoke and Dust* and *In Praise of Carelessness*.

**Fulgentius** (Fifth century A.D.)    Roman writer and philologist. Nothing is known about Fulgentius' life except that he was born in the province of Africa. Among his works are a preposterously allegorical exposition of Virgil's *Aeneid*, a careless study of a number of rare and antiquated Latin words, and the *Mythologiae*, a dialogue in three books between the Greek muse Calliope and the author, who claims to have discovered the true meaning of various myths. Fulgentius' allegorical interpretations are frequently based on fancy if false etymologies. A fourth work, *De Aetatibus Mundi* [On the Ages of the World], is a kind of universal history based primarily on the Bible. In this work, of which fourteen books still survive, Fulgentius employs a bizarre technique called *leipogrammatos:* in the respective books, one letter of the alphabet in succession is not used, a fact declared at the beginning and end of each book.

**Galen** (c. 130–c. 200 A.D.)    Greek physician and medical writer. During his lifetime, Galen conducted an extensive and varied practice. In 158, he served as chief physician to the gladiators in Pergamon (in modern Turkey), a position which gave him experience in techniques of physical training, dietetics, and the treatment of wounds. He was, besides, the personal physician of the emperor Marcus Aurelius and his notorious son Commodus. His contentious disposition, however, his arrogance, and his unveiled contempt for his medical colleagues led to threats of assassination. A key figure in the evolution of modern medicine, Galen was the first to explore physiology and comparative anatomy through the use of dissection and animal experimentation. His work on cranial nerves and the spinal column was extraordinary. Indeed, his prolific writings—more than three hundred treatises—deal with every aspect of the history, theory, and practice of medicine. Galen and his predecessor Hippocrates are the two greatest names in Greek medicine.

**Gaufredi, Raymond**     See **Angelus Clarenus.**

**Gerard of Borgo San Donnino**     See **Spirituals.**

**Gilson, Étienne** (1884–1978)     French Thomistic philosopher who taught at the University of Toronto and the Sorbonne. Perhaps Gilson's greatest contribution to philosophy is his making the works of Thomas Aquinas accessible to modern readers. His definitive work on the system of Aquinas is entitled *The Christian Philosophy of Saint Thomas Aquinas.* He also wrote *The Spirit of Medieval Philosophy, The Unity of Philosophical Experience*, and *The Philosopher and Theology,* an often rambling autobiography that examines the status of the Christian as an intellectual.

**Gui, Bernard** (c. 1261–1331)     Dominican bishop, inquisitor, and historian. Bernard Gui was professed as a Dominican at Limoges and served as prior at Albi, Carcassone, Castres, and Limoges. He was inquisitor at Toulouse from 1307 to 1323, when he was appointed bishop of Tuy in Spain. A man of extraordinary precision, Gui showed a true flare for historical research. The cultivation of an elegant prose style, on the other hand, was far less important to him than the painstaking preservation of numerous facts and relevant evidence. His most famous historical works are the *Flores chronicorum* [The Flowers (the best) of the Chronicles], a universal history, and the *Reges Francorum* [The Kings of the Franks]. His writings on heresy and the Inquisition include a book of reflections on the Inquisition at Toulouse and the *Practica officii inquisitionis,* a handbook on the duties of an inquisitor.

**Hildegarde, Saint** (1098–1179)     German mystic, writer, and pioneer in science. A sickly child given to visions, Hildegarde joined the Benedictine order when she was fifteen. At thirty-eight, she became abbess of Rupertsberg. Her visions grew so numerous in her later life that she was called by her contemporaries "the Sibyl of the Rhine." Her major work, *Scivias* (short for *Nosce vias* [Domini] "know the paths of the Lord"), is a record of twenty-six visions on the Church, Redemption, and man's relation to God, combined with dire apocalyptic warnings. An extraordinarily brilliant woman, Hildegarde wrote hymns, both words and music, allegorical homilies, and books on natural history and medicine, one of which is a treatise on normal and abnormal psychology dealing with such topics as headaches and dizziness, obsessions and insanity—a forerunner, in many ways, of William James' classic, *The Varieties of Religious Experience.* For her own amusement, or perhaps for the communal pleasure of the nuns at Rupertsberg, she created an artificial language containing an alphabet of twenty-three letters and about one thousand words, which seem to be assonant versions of Latin and German words with an unusually large number of final z's.

**Hisperica Famina**     "Elegant sayings," a collection of Latin passages on various subjects (such as sky, wind, sea, fire, prayer, a writing tablet, a hunt, and an encounter with robbers) that was written in southwest Britain in the fifth or sixth century. The product of an esoteric Irish rhetorical school dedicated to the preservation of Latin and Greek learning in the dying days of the Roman Empire, the *Hisperica Famina* contains Latin words so eccentric as to form practically a secret language, like the mysterious writings of Virgil of Toulouse.

**Honorius Augustoduniensis** (c. 1085–c. 1156)     Benedictine philosopher and theologian. Also called Honorius of Autun, he joined the Irish Benedictines at Regensburg. An ardent defender of Christ's Real Presence in the Eucharist and of high moral standards for the clergy, Honorius asserted that a sacrament administered by a priest in the state of mortal sin is valid by the power of Christ; it is invalid, however, if the priest has been excommunicated. He also argued that God is "the substance of all things" beyond the grasp of any creature but containing them all. Everything created is "good," a term identical to "substance," whereas evil is the nothing that is opposed to substance. God's reason for allowing evil in the world is essentially aesthetic: He is the supreme artist who emphasizes and makes more resplendent the good by setting evil in opposition to it.

**Hugh of Newcastle** (c. 1280–after 1322)    Franciscan theologian. Hugh of Newcastle (Novocastro) studied under Duns Scotus at the University of Paris. Between 1307 and 1317, he wrote commentaries on the *Sentences* of Peter Lombard. Hugh of Newcastle attended the Franciscan general chapter in Perugia in 1322 at which the issue of poverty was discussed. He wrote *De victoria Christi contra antichristum* [On Christ's Victory over the Antichrist] and was a staunch defender of the doctrine of the Immaculate Conception.

**Hugh of Saint Victor** (c. 1078–1141)    Saxon philosopher, theologian, and mystical writer. Hugh of Saint Victor was probably related to the noble family of Blankenburg in Saxony. Around 1115, he entered the newly founded Abbey of Saint Victor in Paris. Hugh wrote innumerable works on such varied subjects as angels, sacraments, methods of prayer, techniques of studying, the distinction between philosophy and theology, and the divisions and history of all the sciences. In logic, he followed, for the most part, Aristotle and Boethius. In physics, Hugh asserted that matter had an atomic structure, and he regarded fire as the most sublime of the four elements on the assumption that it united matter to spirit. Hugh of Saint Victor is perhaps most famous, however, for his classic definition of faith as "a certainty about things absent, above opinion and below science."

**Humbert of Romans** (c. 1194–1277)    Dominican master general. Humbert became a Dominican in 1224 and later served as provincial of both the Roman and French provinces. Finally, in 1254, he was elected the fifth master general of the Order of Preachers (Dominicans), an office he held for nine years before resigning. Besides supervising the revision of the Dominican liturgy, Humbert wrote works of ascetical theology and encyclical letters clarifying the mission and spirit of the Dominican order.

**Ibn al-Alkami** The last vizir of Baghdad, who owned one of the largest libraries of that city. The library, which contained 10,000 books, was destroyed during the sack of Baghdad by the Mongols in 1258, when every one of Baghdad's thirty-six libraries also perished.

**Ibn Hazm** (994–1064) Andalusian poet, psychologist, philosopher, and theologian. Ibn Hazm, who spent his early childhood in a harem, wrote a fascinating treatise on love and lovers and on the apparent and hidden meaning of lovers' words. He also wrote perceptive comments on feminine psychology. In his *Kitab al-Takrib*, Ibn Hazm gives a summary of Aristotelian logic and in his *Kitab al-Muhalla*, an analysis of prophecy, Paradise, and Hell. Linguistic theoretician and moralist both, Ibn Hazm stated that the evil of liars is that they use language for their own ends instead of serving it. Language has been instituted by God and contains in itself a truth. It is itself, moreover, the only means of discovering the truth and of expressing it, provided it is not removed from its divine origins to become the pawn of human desires.

**Isa ibn-Ali** (Eleventh century) Arab medical writer. Influenced by the writings of the Greek physician Galen, Isa ibn-Ali was the greatest oculist of the Arabs. His work *Tadhkirat al-Kahhalin* or *De oculis* [On the Eyes] is the earliest extant Arabic work on ophthalmology. Divided into three books, the treatise covers the anatomy of the eye (Book 1), externally visible diseases of the eye, such as cataracts and conjunctivitis, and their treatment (Book 2), and hidden diseases of the eye, such as myopia, farsightedness, and strabismus, and their treatment (Book 3). The work ends with 141 simple remedies arranged in alphabetical order.

**Isidore of Seville** (c. 560–636)    Archbishop and writer. Isidore was educated in a monastery by his brother, whom he succeeded as archbishop of Seville in 599/600. Isidore, a giant of erudition, was instrumental in raising the academic standards for priestly ordination and setting up cathedral schools in every diocese of Spain. He wrote innumerable works, the most important of which are the *Historia de regibus Gothorum* [History of the Kings of the Goths], one of the principal sources for the history of the Visigoths, and the *Etymologiae* [Etymologies] or *Origins*. The latter, an encyclopedic survey of all knowledge in twenty books, contains historical, descriptive, and anecdotal information on a great variety of subjects—the seven liberal arts, geography, foods, drinks, precious stones, law, medicine, and natural history, among others. A cornucopia of delectable trivia, the *Etymologiae* was one of the most popular textbooks of the Middle Ages. The cathedral library of Seville, moreover, contains an ingenious poem apparently written by Isidore describing the contents of a library, its authors and their characteristics.

**Joachim of Calabria** (c. 1135–1202)    Cistercian mystic and theologian. Also known as Joachim of Fiore or Floris, Joachim made a pilgrimage to the Holy Land which changed his life. Upon his return, he lived as a hermit on Mt. Etna and then engaged in lay preaching until he was forced by ecclesiastical disapproval to take his vows at the monastery of Corazzo, where he was ordained in 1168 and later became abbot. Through Joachim's efforts, Corazzo, a Benedictine house, was incorporated into the stricter Cistercian order. But by the time of its incorporation, Joachim had already left the now austere Cistercians at Corazzo to found in Fiore an even more rigorous branch of the order: an action that resulted in his denunciation as a renegade by the Cistercian General Chapter. Despite this, by the time of his death, Joachim had become one of the most respected religious figures of the day.

Joachim's three major works are the *Exposition on the Apocalypse*, the *Concordance of the New and Old Testament*, and the *Ten-Stringed Psaltery*. In these lengthy, repetitious, pseudo-prophetical works, Joachim developed a Trinitarian philosophy of history, according to which history progresses through three stages of increasing spirituality: the ages of the Father, the Son, and the Holy Spirit. Joachim's deeply pessimistic, apocalyptic doctrines were embraced by the Franciscan Spirituals who carried them far beyond Joachim's intentions.

**John XXII** (c. 1249–1334)   Born Jacques d'Euse of Cahors, he taught canon and civil law at Cahors and Toulouse. Shortly after his election to the papacy, John took action against the Franciscan Spirituals, who raised the question of evangelical poverty and were persecuted for their stand. He went so far as to imprison a delegation that came to him at Avignon, and three of John XXII's most famous bulls were directed against them. In *Quorundam exigit* (1317), John commanded the Franciscan Spirituals to abandon their short habits and to obey their former superiors. In *Sancta Romana* (1317), he condemned the Fraticelli and the Beguines. His *Gloriosam ecclesiam* (1318) denounced the Tuscan Spirituals who had fled to Sicily. In 1322, the Pope, whose fondness for ermine was notorious, attacked the Franciscan doctrine of absolute evangelical poverty. He issued four bulls on the subject of ownership—*Ad conditorem canonum* (1322), *Cum inter nonnullos* (1323), *Quia quorundam mentes* (1324), and *Quia vir reprobus* (1329)—that declared it heretical to assert that Christ and His disciples had not owned the goods that the New Testament said they had possessed.

**John of Jandun** (c. 1275–1328)   Averroist philosopher and teacher at Paris. A close friend of Marsilius of Padua, John proudly proclaimed himself "a mimic of Aristotle and Averroes." He wrote commentaries on Averroes' *De substantia orbis* [On the

Substance of the World] and on Aristotle's *Physics, Metaphysics, Parva naturalia*, and *De anima*. John embraced the principal teachings of Averroes, particularly the eternity of the world, the unicity of the human intellect, i.e. only one intellect in each person, and the denial of personal immortality. He worked with Marsilius on the writing of *Defensor pacis* [Defender of the Peace] and was consequently compelled to leave Paris. In 1326, he took refuge with Louis IV of Bavaria, along with Marsilius of Padua, Michael of Cesena, and William of Occam. The next year John XXII condemned many of the propositions in *Defensor pacis*, mentioning John of Jandun by name in the bull of condemnation.

**John of Salisbury** (c. 1115–1180)    English scholar, philosopher, and humanist. Born in Salisbury, John studied in Paris under Peter Abelard and was a friend of Bernard of Clairvaux and Thomas Becket. His two major works are the *Metalogicon* and the *Polycraticus*, both of which he completed in 1159. The *Metalogicon*, a study of Aristotelian logic, is both a defense of the *trivium* (grammar, dialectic, and rhetoric) and an attack on formal Scholasticism. The *Polycraticus* or *Statesman's Guide* (subtitled *Frivolities of Courtiers and Footprints of Philosophers)* was dedicated to Thomas Becket. It is a treatise on church and state government which proposes a society in which temporal power is delegated by the church to the ruler. John of Salisbury also wrote a life of Thomas Becket and was, in fact, with Archbishop Becket on the day of his murder in the cathedral.

**Kempis, Thomas à**    See **Thomas à Kempis.**

**Kircher, Athanasius** (1601–1680)    Jesuit scientist, archaeologist, and linguist. Admitted as a novice to the Jesuit College at Paderborn in 1618, Kircher moved to Rome in 1635, where he taught physics, mathematics, and Oriental languages. A scientific genius, Kircher is credited with the construction of convergent mirrors and of a sophisticated magic lantern with convex lens to focus images more sharply on the screen—the prototype of the modern film projector. He also invented the world's first calculator, built a powerful megaphone, and was the first person to use the expansion of mercury to measure changes in temperature. In 1638, in order to witness the activities and measure the depth of the volcano Stromboli, the insatiable polymath had himself lowered by a rope into the crater. In his later life, he divided his energies between physics and archaeology. Two of his principal works reflect his interests—*Ars magna lucis et umbrae* [The Great Art of Light and Shade], written in 1645, and *Lingua aegyptica restituta* [The Egyptian Language Restored], a treatise on the decipherment of hieroglyphs.

**Lucan** (39–65 A.D.)    Roman epic poet born at Corduba in Spain. The nephew of Seneca, Nero's tutor, Lucan was forced to commit suicide for joining the conspiracy of Piso against the emperor Nero. At his death, he left an unfinished historical epic, in 9½ books, entitled the *Pharsalia* or *De bello civili*. The poem, brilliantly epigrammatic if occasionally boring, concerns the civil war between Julius Caesar and Pompey.

**Lucian of Samosata**    See **Apuleius of Madaura.**

**Luciferines**    The adherents of Lucifer of Cagliari (died c. 370). Lucifer was a fanatical defender of the innovative Trinitarian teachings of the Council of Nicaea. He directed his violent invective not only against his opponents but even against those who simply questioned his teachings. That Lucifer eventually died a schismatic is confirmed by the writings of Saint Augustine and Saint Ambrose. Among those opposed to his teachings was Saint Jerome, who lashed out against the Luciferines in his *Dialogus contra Luciferianos*.

**Lyons, Second Council of** (1274)    The Second Council of Lyons was called in 1274 by Pope Gregory X who wished to effect clerical reform, reunite the Latin and Greek churches, and promote a crusade to the Holy Land. Not surprisingly, the issue of clerical reform involved lengthy and heated debates. In the end, restrictions were placed on most orders, with the exception of the Franciscans and Dominicans. More than two hundred prelates attended the council, among them, Bonaventure of Bagnoregio, who died during one of the sessions. Thomas Aquinas died on his way to the meetings.

**Mabillon, Jean** (1632–1707)    Benedictine scholar and hagiographer. Jean Mabillon entered the Benedictines in 1654. His principal work is the *Acta Sanctorum ordinis sancti Benedicti* [Deeds of the Saints of the Order of Saint Benedict], a nine-volume collection of writings from 500–1100 that document the lives of Benedictine saints. In 1675, the first of the four volumes of the *Vetera analecta* was published. A heated argument in 1691 with Abbot de Rancé of La Trappe, who insisted that monks should engage in manual labor rather than study, led to Mabillon's famous defense of monastic learning, *Tractatus de studiis monasticis* [Treatise on Monastic Studies]. In it, Mabillon attempted to reconstruct the contents of the library at Vivarium, a monastery in Calabria founded around 540 by Cassiodorus, from the evidence of Cassiodorus' own works. He also wrote a controversial work, *De cultu sanctorum ignotorum* [On the Cult of Unknown Saints], in which he attacked the practice of venerating unidentified relics from the catacombs. The short book was denounced to the Holy Office, and Mabillon was ordered to clarify some of his statements and to retract others. Again, in 1700, Mabillon's preface to the Maurist edition of St. Augustine aroused such a storm that Mabillon was accused of heresy, but he was eventually exonerated by the Holy Office.

**Map, Walter** (c. 1140–c. 1210)    Anglo-Norman ecclesiastic and satirist. In 1179, after several years in the Chancellorship of London, Walter Map was made Archdeacon of Oxford. During his lifetime, Map enjoyed a considerable reputation as a wit and satirist. He is the author of *De nugis curialium* [On the Trifles of the Courtiers], a prose miscellany of legends, homilies, gossip, and satire that throws light on Anglo-Norman history, particularly on the reign of King Henry II of England. In addition, a large body of satirical poetry, much of it directed against ecclesiastical follies, has been attributed to Map, who was a notoriously severe critic of the Cistercians.

**Margaret of Città di Castello, Blessed** (1287–1320)    Italian mystic. Born in Metola, she is sometimes called Margaret of Metola. According to one account, Margaret was so severely handicapped (she was blind, lame, dwarfed, and hunchbacked) that her aristocratic parents hid her until she was sixteen. Then, hoping for a miracle, they took their daughter to a popular shrine in Città di Castello; but when no miracle occurred, they abandoned her there. According to another account, Margaret was already a foundling by the age of six and was raised in a convent of worldly nuns who regarded her blameless conduct as a tacit rebuke to their disregard of the rule. Neglected, persecuted, and finally forced to leave, Margaret devoted herself to tending the sick and the dying. Despite her disabilities, she also ministered tirelessly to prisoners in the city jail and taught the village children psalms and catechism while their parents were at work. Margaret is said to have enjoyed the gift of levitation: while praying, she often floated more than a foot above the ground. Most medievalists contend that the devout mystic of Città di Castello praised by Ubertino of Casale in his *Arbor vitae crucifixae Jesu* [The Tree of the Crucified Life of Jesus] is Margaret.

**Marsilius of Padua** (c. 1275–1342)    Political philosopher. In 1313, Marsilius of Padua was made rector of the University of Paris where, in 1324, he completed *Defensor pacis* [Defender of the Peace], his one major work and one of the most original documents on political theory written during the Middle Ages. Highly critical of papal politics, Marsilius argued that the source of all political power is the people and that the power of the church must be limited to preserve and protect the unity of the state. When Marsilius' authorship of the controversial antipapal treatise became known, he had to leave Paris. He sought the protection of Louis IV of Bavaria, an avowed enemy of John XXII. In 1328, the Roman people made Louis IV emperor, denounced John XXII as a heretic, and installed a Franciscan dissident named Pietro Rainalducci as anti-pope Nicholas V. Shortly afterwards, the fickle mob tired of their new emperor and forced him to leave Rome. Marsilius accompanied Louis IV back to Germany where he spent the rest of his life. Marsilius of Padua has been called the precursor of the Protestant reformation and a prophet of both totalitarianism and modern democracy. *Defensor pacis* was translated into English in 1536 to lend support to the actions of Henry VIII.

**Martianus Capella** (Fifth century A.D.)     Latin encyclopedist. Born in Carthage, Martianus Capella was a lawyer who, in his later years, wrote an elaborate work in prose and verse entitled *On the Marriage of Mercury and Philology*. A weird and tedious allegory, the work is divided into nine books, the first two of which are devoted to the married couple—Mercury and a beautiful young nymph of great learning, Philology. The next seven books describe the seven bridesmaids, personifications of the Seven Liberal Arts—the Trivium (Grammar, Dialectic, Rhetoric) and Quadrivium (Geometry, Astronomy, Arithmetic, Music).

**Melk, Abbey of**     The Abbey of Melk is a Benedictine monastery on the right bank of the Danube in lower Austria. It is forty-four miles west of Vienna. Founded in 1089, the monastery and its library were destroyed by a fire in 1297. It was enlarged and fortified in the fourteenth century, gutted again in 1683, and rebuilt from 1702 to 1736. During his victorious campaign against Austria in 1805–1809, Napoleon established his headquarters at Melk. Today there are about forty monks at Melk, most of whom teach at the local liberal arts *gymnasium* or do parish work.

The library of Melk still has 75,000 volumes, 1800 manuscripts, and 800 incunabula.

**Michael of Cesena** (c. 1270–1342)    Franciscan minister general and theologian. Working with Pope John XXII, Michael of Cesena managed to ease the tension between the Franciscan Spirituals and the rest of the Franciscan community. Indeed, most of the rebels submitted once again to his authority. Ubertino of Casale and Angelus Clarenus, on the other hand, left the order. In 1319, Michael secured the condemnation of Pierre Olieu's work on the Apocalypse, which had been an inspiration to the Spirituals.

The breach of friendship between Michael and John XXII finally occurred in 1322, when the pope condemned the Franciscan doctrine of absolute evangelical poverty. The order responded by reaffirming it at a general chapter in Perugia the same year. John's subsequent bulls—*Ad conditorem canonum, Cum inter nonnullos,* and *Quia quorundam*—which made it heretical to declare the absolute poverty of Christ and his disciples infuriated the Franciscans. They became more friendly toward Louis IV of Bavaria, who had been excommunicated by John. In 1327, Michael of Cesena was summoned to Avignon. Soon afterwards, he fled from Avignon with William of Occam and Bonagratia of Bergamo (died 1347). Michael's alliance with Louis IV eventually led to his expulsion from the Franciscan order in 1331. An extraordinarily complex man, Michael died unsubmissive, having entrusted his writings to Queen Sanchia of Naples.

**Minorites**    Another name for the *Friars Minor* ("inferior brothers") who belong to the branch of the Franciscan order that follows literally the rule of Saint Francis. "Minorites" is a term that emphasizes their humility.

**The Number of the Beast**    The Number of the Beast is 666, a mystical number that refers to a man mentioned by John in the Book of Revelation (13:18). Among numerologists and

Cabbalists, every letter of the alphabet represents a number. A person's "number" is the sum of the numerical equivalents to the letters in his or her name.

**Occam, William of** (c. 1285–1349)     Franciscan philosopher and theologian. William of Occam (also, Ockham) entered the Franciscan order and studied at Oxford, where he lectured on the Bible and the *Sentences* of Peter Lombard from 1315 to 1319. In 1324, he was summoned to appear before Pope John XXII at Avignon to answer charges about his commentary on the *Sentences*, but he was not condemned. William was also involved in the dispute about evangelical poverty and, in May 1328, was forced to flee from Avignon with the Franciscan general, Michael of Cesena. He joined King Louis IV of Bavaria at Pisa and accompanied him to Munich. Thenceforth Occam participated more actively in the struggle between Louis and the pope regarding secular and ecclesiastical power. This led to his excommunication and expulsion from the Franciscan order. When Louis died in 1347, Occam attempted to reconcile himself with the pope, but it is not known whether any reconciliation was ever effected.

Occam wrote many philosophical, theological, and political treatises, including the *Summa* (*totius*) *logicae* and the *Quaestiones in octo libros physicorum*. Occam rejected the view that universals (general concepts) have an independent existence. According to Occam, only individual things exist. There cannot be existent universals. Universals are terms that signify individual things and that stand for them in propositions. Their universality is purely functional. Occam denied the existence outside the mind of a common nature possessed by many individual things. To assert the existence of universals outside the mind is to assert a contradiction. For if a universal exists, it must be, like any reality, singular and unique.

**Odo of Cluny, Saint** (c. 879–942)     Second abbot of Cluny. Odo had already received the tonsure—the shaving of a cleric's head—by the time he was nineteen. His industry and humility attracted the attention of Berno, the first abbot of the newly founded Cluny. Berno had Odo ordained and then, in 927, chosen as his successor as abbot of Cluny. Odo led Cluny to great holiness and worked for the reform of several monasteries in France and Italy.

**Old Man of the Mountain**     Title of Hasan ibn-al-Sabbah, or Hassan ben Sabbah, founder of the Assassins, a band of Moslem terrorists, whose strongholds were in the mountains of Lebanon. The name "Assassins" (or *Hashishin*) is derived from their reputed habit of taking hashish before their murderous attacks on the Seljuks, the Turkish rulers of Persia, Syria, and Asia Minor before the Ottomans, or on Christians in the time of the Crusades.

**Olieu, Pierre** (1248–1298)     Franciscan philosopher and theologian. After earning a bachelor's degree in theology, Pierre Olieu (or Peter John Olivi) ended his formal studies, since he regarded the pursuit of further academic honors incompatible with his life as a humble Franciscan friar. Instead he applied himself to severe asceticism and writing. A strict observer of the Franciscan rule, especially of evangelical poverty, Olieu won the fanatical admiration of the Franciscan Spirituals. In 1285, at the general chapter of Milan, Olieu was accused of leading a dangerously insubordinate sect. He was also summoned to appear before the general chapters of the Franciscans at Montpelier in 1287 and at Paris in 1292 to explain his position on Franciscan poverty. Each time he escaped condemnation. The saintly Olieu spent his final years at Narbonne.

**Pachomius, Saint** (292–346)     Born in the Upper Thebaid in Egypt, Pachomius was a soldier in the imperial army—a profession he abandoned when he embraced Christianity. For a while, he lived on bread and salt as a hermit, but later, he gathered around himself communities of Christian ascetics and wrote the first cenobitical rule. By the time of his death, there were more than three thousand monks in nine monasteries under his rule.

**Paracelsus** (1493–1541)    Swiss physician and alchemist. His real name was Theophrastus Philippus Aureolus Bombastus von Hohenheim. But when he was in his mid-thirties, he adopted the pseudonym "Paracelsus," which was either a boastful allusion ("better than Celsus") to the ancient Roman physician Celsus or a Latinization of his name Hohenheim, or both. Most of Paracelsus' medical theories are discounted today. Intensely religious, he contended that man was composed of three elements, salt, sulphur, and mercury, and embodied three aspects, physical, spiritual, and divine. On the other hand, Paracelsus rejected the popular medieval notion of disease as an imbalance of bodily humors and maintained that diseases were separate entities introduced into the body by external agents. Eccentric, irascible, and insanely egotistical, Paracelsus helped to undermine the authoritarian approach to medicine of the late Middle Ages and to pave the way for more scientific methods of observation and free inquiry.

**Pastoureaux**    The Pastoureaux were roving bands of discontented peasants and shepherds who passed through France in 1251 on their way to the Holy Land. Their goal was to free King Louis IX of France from the Moslems and to recapture Jerusalem. The Pastoureaux were led by a charismatic preacher in his sixties, the "Master of Hungary," who spoke French, Flemish, and Latin and carried with him a map which he said had been given to him by the Virgin Mary. The Pastoureaux desecrated churches and engaged in violent activities against feudal lords and the clergy, especially the Franciscans and Dominicans, whom, for some reason, they blamed for the misfortunes that plagued Louis' Crusade in Egypt. The Pastoureaux were soon suppressed by order of Blanche of Castile, the Queen-Regent. The mysterious "Master of Hungary" died in battle, and not more than a handful of the Pastoureaux reached the Holy Land.

**Patarines**    A movement of laity and lower clergy that arose in northern Italy in the eleventh century, the Patarines directed their attacks mainly against the upper classes and the higher clergy. They condemned simony, denounced priests' concubinage and marriage, and, in Milan, refused to receive the sacraments from corrupt ecclesiastics. The more militant of the Patarines, indeed, went so far as to remove forcibly from the altar any priest they deemed unworthy of his calling. Regarded by most bishops as a dangerous sect subversive of hierarchical authority, the Patarines may in fact have signalled a growing desire on the part of the laity to engage more fully in the life of the church.

**Paulicians**    A dualist sect that first appeared in Armenia in the seventh century. The Paulicians believed in two gods: the good God, the creator of souls and the Lord of heaven, and the evil God, the Demiurge, the creator and ruler of the material universe. Convinced that matter was evil, the Paulicians denied the reality of Christ's body and His redemption. They rejected the cross, relics, and icons, downgraded the sacraments of Baptism and the Eucharist, and repudiated marriage and the priesthood. The Byzantine Emperor Alexius I Comnenus suppressed the sect, but traces of it are evident in the Bogomils of Bulgaria.

**Paulinus of Nola, Saint** (c. 353–431)    Christian Latin writer. Born of a wealthy Gallo-Roman family in Bordeaux, Paulinus was the favorite pupil of the writer Ausonius. He married a Spanish woman, Therasia, and later moved to Spain with his wife and son. The saintly Paulinus and his family were so loved by the people that he was ordained by the bishop of Barcelona and was eventually made bishop of Nola. His writings include fifty-one letters, many of which are addressed to his friend and teacher Ausonius, and thirty-three perfectly crafted poems. Especially noteworthy is Paulinus' epithalamium for Bishop Julian of Eclanum, one of the earliest Christian wedding poems.

The first reference to a Bible reading room, open to all, occurs in one of Paulinus' letters. While noting the erection of a church at Nola, Paulinus mentions a *Secretum* or "reading room," describing in detail the room and the verses that adorned its walls.

**Peter of Morrone**     See **Celestine V.**

**Phalaris, bull of**     Perillus, an Athenian artist, made a hollow brazen bull for Phalaris, the tyrant of Agrigentum in Sicily (c. 570–554 B.C.). Phalaris, notorious for cruelty, confined his victims in the bull and roasted them alive. To test the invention, Phalaris ordered Perillus himself to be shut up in the bull and baked to death.

**Philadelphia, the angel of**     Philadelphia is one of the seven cities of Asia whose church is visited by an angel in the Book of Revelation (chapters 1–3). The other cities are Ephesus, Smyrna, Pergamos, Thyatira, Sardis, and Laodicea.

**Physiologus**     Among the most important of Christian didactic works in the Middle Ages, the *Physiologus* is a collection of fanciful descriptions of real and imaginary animals, birds, and even minerals that serve to throw light on Christian doctrine. The name *Physiologus* probably referred originally to the anonymous pagan author of a pseudoscientific work which simply contained the characteristics of various animals. Eventually the name was applied to the work itself. Finally a Christian writer, no less anonymous than his pagan predecessor, added the allegorical material. In its present form, the *Physiologus* reveals the influence of Isidore of Seville, Solinus, and Pliny the Elder.

**Pierre of Maricourt** (Thirteenth century, *floruit* 1261–69) French scholastic and scientist. Pierre of Maricourt was the teacher of Roger Bacon, who considered him the greatest mathematician of his day and the one man who could be praised enthusiastically and without qualification for his achievements in experimental research. Pierre wrote a treatise on the astrolabe and a fascinating letter on the magnet, in which he not only presents the theory of magnetism but describes in detail three instruments that he invented for magnetic experiments. He also worked for at least three years on the manufacture of a mirror which would produce combustion at a distance.

**Platearius** (Eleventh/twelfth centuries)     Surname of three generations of physicians living in Salerno. Among their works are the *Practica brevis* [Short Manual], a medical compendium, *Regulae urinarum*, a treatise on urology, and *De simplici medicina,* which is extremely important from a botanical point of view, since 229 of its 273 chapters deal with medicinal plants.

**Pliny the Elder** (23–79 A.D.)     Roman natural historian, grammarian, and administrator. Pliny the Elder held a number of military and naval posts, including that of commander of the Roman fleet at Misenum in 79 A.D. While conducting rescue operations and attempting to gain first-hand knowledge of volcanoes, he was suffocated by ashes from Mt. Vesuvius. His lost works include a treatise on the use of javelins, a work on diction, and a *History of the German Wars.* His only work to survive is the monumental *Natural History* in thirty-seven books, which embraces astronomy, meteorology, geography, anthropology, physiology, zoology, botany, medicine, and mineralogy. Although much of Pliny's information is untrustworthy, the *Natural History* was extremely influential during the Middle Ages and is even today a valuable source for ancient learning.

**Pliny the Younger** (61/62-c. 114 A.D.)     Roman writer and statesman. Educated by the rhetorician Quintilian, Pliny the Younger became the emperor Trajan's special legate to the province of Bithynia. He is most famous for his lively and engaging correspondence—ten books of informal social history that touch on court activity, literature, Roman life and manners, current events, and geography. Especially noteworthy are his accounts of early Christians and of the last days of Pompeii, in which his uncle, Pliny the Elder, perished.

**Poor Lombards**     See **Waldensians**.

**Poor of Lyons, the**     See **Waldensians**.

**Prester John**     Prester (Presbyter) John was a fabulous figure in medieval legend—variously called the Christian emperor of Asia, the lord of the Tartars (in Marco Polo's *Travels*), or the Emperor of Ethiopia or Abyssinia. Prester John's realm supposedly contained a fountain moved from Mt. Olympus, the abode of the Greek gods. To drink from it three times while fasting preserved the drinker from infirmity and old age. He would always have the appearance of a thirty-year-old. Prester John's palace had gates of sardonyx, a court paved with onyx, and a sapphire couch on which he slept to keep himself chaste. Eagles fetched stones which, when worn on the finger, would restore a blind man's sight. Prester John himself owned magical stones that were able to control the weather and to turn water into milk or wine. Louis IV of Bavaria sarcastically referred to John XXII as "Prester John."

**Prudentius** (348–410)     Christian Latin poet. Born in northern Spain, Prudentius dedicated his talents as a poet to the Church. His major works include the *Peristephanon* [On the Crowns], fourteen magnificent if gory poems in honor of the martyrs, especially the Spanish, the *Psychomachia* [The Battle for the Soul of Man], an allegorical epic of the struggle between the forces of good and evil within the soul of man, and the *Cathemerinon* [The Diary], a collection of hymns for the various hours of the day as well as for different feast days and religious ceremonies.

**Psellus, Michael** (1018–1096/97)    Byzantine philosopher, historian, and humanist. Michael Psellus was born in Constantinople. After gaining a reputation as a child prodigy, he entered a monastery in Asia Minor, but left when he realized that he did not have a religious vocation. Instead he devoted his life and energies to study and writing. His voluminous writings include manuals of rhetoric and discussions of problems in medicine, meteorology, and astronomy. Two of his most famous works are the *Chronography*, a history—clever, cruel, and eminently readable—of the years 976 to 1078, and *De omnifaria doctrina* [On Knowledge of All Sorts], a compilation of 193 answers to various questions—scientific, philosophical, and theological—raised by his students and friends.

**Pseudo-Apostles**    See **Dolcino of Novara (Fra)**.

**Ptolemy** (c. 100–170 A.D.)    Greek astronomer, mathematician, and geographer who lived in Alexandria, Egypt. Among his most famous works are the *Geographikē Hyphēgēsis*, a geographical primer in eight books, which gives the latitudes and longitudes of about 8000 places and explains how to use these calculations in order to draw maps; the *Tetrabiblos*, an astrological treatise in four books; and the *Almagest*, a mathematical treatment of astronomical phenomena. The *Almagest*, which derives its name from a ninth-century Arabic translation, is divided into thirteen books. It contains a catalogue of the stars and treats, among other things, the relations of the earth and heavens, solar and lunar eclipses, the movement of the planets, the motion of the sun and the length of the year. The *Almagest* presents a geocentric conception of the universe that would dominate European astronomy until the coming of the heliocentric system of Copernicus in the sixteenth century.

**Quintilian** (35/40–c. 100 A.D.)    Roman educator, rhetorician, and literary critic. Quintilian was born at Calagurris in Spain, but received his education in Rome. With his appointment as public professor of rhetoric by the emperor Vespasian, he became the first government-paid teacher in the history of Europe. Among his pupils were Pliny the Younger and the emperor Domitian's two grandnephews. His treatise, the *Institutio Oratoria* [The Training of an Orator] in twelve books, was probably intended as a program for the education of the young princes and of Quintilian's own children. This work had a profound influence on Renaissance and 17th-century educational theory and literary criticism.

**Rabanus (Hrabanus) Maurus, Blessed** (780–856)     Frankish churchman, Abbot of Fulda, Latin theologian and poet. Rabanus Maurus studied under the great Carolingian scholar Alcuin, who considered him his most brilliant pupil. From 822 to 842, Rabanus was abbot of Fulda, the most influential German monastery of its day. Under Rabanus, the school and library became extremely important. In 842, he resigned to devote more of his energies to study. Five years later he was appointed archbishop of Mainz. Disturbed by the specter of a civilization that appeared to be disintegrating before his eyes, Rabanus wished to preserve and propagate the wisdom of the past. His own literary output was immense. It included works as various as an encyclopedia entitled *De Universo* modelled on the *Etymologiae* of Isidore of Seville, a work on calculations of the calendar, a short treatise entitled *On the Invention of Languages* which reflects Rabanus' delight in runes and symbols, theological tracts on the education of the clergy and marriages between blood relatives, and a poem, *De Laudibus Sanctae Crucis* [On the Praises of the Holy Cross], in which verses are ingeniously superimposed on a drawing so that the letters along its outline form words or sentences.

**Robertus Anglicus** (Twelfth century)     Robertus Anglicus ("Robert the Englishman") is Robert of Chester, also known as Robert of Ketene, an important figure in the history of Arabic learning in England. In 1143, he completed a translation of the

Koran from Arabic. He also translated from Arabic to Latin the *Judgments* of Alkindi, the *Algebra* of Al-Kuwarizmi, and a treatise on alchemy. His original contributions to medieval science include a treatise on the astrolabe and a set of astronomical tables for the meridian of London in 1149–50.

**Roger of Hereford** (Twelfth century)    Roger was a canon of Hereford which, at this time, was the chief center in England for the study of science. Roger wrote several astronomical works, including a treatise on the planets, one on the rising and setting of constellations, a work comparing Latin and Hebrew calendars, and *De rebus metallicis*. He also compiled a set of astronomical tables for the meridian of Hereford in 1178.

**Sachsenhausen Appellation**    An edict of King Louis IV of Bavaria, issued on May 22, 1324, in which he accused Pope John XXII of heresy because of his bulls against evangelical poverty.

**Sciopods** (or **Sciapodes** "shadow feet")    A mythical people in Libya whose feet had monstrously large soles which they were said to turn up and use as umbrellas. They are mentioned by, among others, Pliny the Elder in his *Natural History* and Saint Augustine in his *City of God*.

**Silius Italicus** (c. 25-c. 100A.D.)    Roman art collector, bibliophile, and poet. Silius Italicus wrote the *Punica*, an epic poem in seventeen books on the Second Punic War. Over 12,000 lines long, it is the longest and perhaps most dismal poem in Latin literature—a poem that Pliny the Younger said was written *maiore cura quam ingenio* ("with more pains than talent"). To shorten an incurable illness, Silius Italicus deliberately starved himself to death in a house once owned by Rome's greatest poet, Virgil.

**Solinus, Gaius Julius** (Third century A.D.)    Roman writer. Solinus was the author of the *Collectanea rerum memorabilium* [Collections of memorable facts], most of which was taken directly from the *Natural History* of Pliny. Better known by its later title, *Polyhistor,* a name given in the sixth century or in the third century by the author himself to a second edition of his work, the book is a geographical survey of the known world, with preposterous remarks on the origins, history, strange tribes, customs, animals, and monsters of various countries. Solinus' slavish dependence on the *Natural History* has earned him the title of "Pliny's Ape." It was Solinus, incidentally, who coined the term *mare Mediterraneum* (Mediterranean Sea).

**Speculum Stultorum** ("A Mirror for Fools")     Composed between November 1179 and March 1180 by a Benedictine monk named Nigellus Wireker, the *Speculum Stultorum* is a satirical animal fable in Latin dedicated to William de Longchamps, Bishop of Ely, in England. The hero of the poem, Brunellus, or Burnellus, an ass dissatisfied with the length of his tail, represents the monk or ecclesiastic who is discontented with his lot and aspires to the office of prior, abbot, or bishop. To increase the size of his tail, Brunellus travels from Cremona, where he escapes from his master, to Salerno, Lyons, and Paris, and back to Cremona again. Valuable for its vivid insights into student life at Paris during the twelfth century, the *Speculum Stultorum* is most inspired when it lampoons mercilessly the vices and follies of monastic orders, bishops, pastors, the Roman Curia, princes, indeed, of all classes of society. Its influence can be seen in Chaucer, Boccaccio, and John Gower.

**Spirituals**     The Spirituals, or Franciscan Spirituals, were strict, uncompromising observers of the rule and spirit of Saint Francis of Assisi. They embraced wholeheartedly the millennarian doctrines of Joachim of Calabria (Fiore) on the coming "age of the Holy Spirit"—an apocalyptic age preceded by the advent of the Antichrist and ushered in by a band of barefooted contemplatives, whom they imagined to be themselves. The condemnation in 1254 of Gerard of Borgo San Donnino's *Introduction to the Eternal Gospel,* viewed by many Spirituals as the

Bible of the new era, as well as the Franciscan order's increasingly relaxed attitude toward poverty broadened the gap between the Spirituals and the rest of the Franciscan community. Eventually, in 1318, four recalcitrant Spirituals were burned at Marseilles for refusing to abandon their skimpy habits.

**Stagirite, the** Title of Aristotle, Greek philosopher and scientist, who was born at Stagira in 384 B.C.

**Statius** (c. 45–c. 96 A.D.) Roman epic poet. Statius was born in Naples. His principal work is the *Thebaid*, an erudite, slightly overdone epic poem in twelve books on the expedition of the Seven against Thebes and the duel to the death of Oedipus' sons, Eteocles and Polyneices. Statius devoted a dozen years to the writing of the *Thebaid*. He also wrote an unfinished epic, the *Achilleid*, whose subject was to have been the life of the Greek warrior Achilles and his death in the Trojan War. Cut short by Statius' death, the poem ends abruptly in the second of a projected twelve books. Perhaps because it lacks the author's scrupulous revisions, the *Achilleid* is crisper and more lively than the *Thebaid*. Statius also wrote the *Silvae*—a miscellany of thirty-two engaging if somewhat oblique poems on subjects such as birthdays, weddings, deaths, favorite pets and slaves, works of art, sleep, and the emperor Domitian's hospitality and his greatness as a road-builder.

**Sulpicius Severus** (c. 360–425) Christian ecclesiastical writer and hagiographer. Born in Aquitania, Sulpicius Severus became a presbyter on the advice of Martin of Tours. He wrote the *Chronica* [Universal History], which begins with the Creation and proceeds by way of the Old and New Testaments to the consulship of Stilicho and Aurelianus in 400 A.D. and the great persecutions and heresies of the late Roman Empire. Sulpicius Severus also wrote the first best seller of the Middle Ages, *The Life of Saint Martin of Tours*. The book was an overnight success, and the booksellers were unable to keep up with the demand for it. Sulpicius Severus' friend Paulinus took a copy with him to Rome, where the booksellers were soon ecstatic over the rapid sales. It was also a success in Alexandria.

**Symphosius** (c. Fifth century A.D.)   Latin writer. Symphosius is the author of one hundred versified riddles that appear in the African Anthology, a collection of short Latin poems edited towards the end of the Vandal domination of Africa in the fifth century A.D. Symphosius' riddles influenced the Anglo-Saxon books of riddles and especially Aldhelm of Malmesbury.

**Synesius of Cyrene** (c. 370–c. 415)   Greek Neoplatonist, bishop, scientist, and writer. Synesius studied philosophy, astronomy, and mathematics under the Neoplatonist Hypatia, who was murdered by fanatical Christians in 415. Synesius' wife and brother were Christians, and he himself converted to the Christian faith and was elected bishop. His letters, 156 of which still survive, constitute both an autobiography of the erudite and charitable Synesius and a penetrating social history of the times. Synesius also wrote *The Egyptian Tale, or On Providence*, in which he describes events in the life of his patron Aurelianus under the allegorical guise of the struggle between the gods Osiris and Typhon. Synesius composed a treatise *On Dreams*, in which he discusses their prophetic value, a number of hymns, and a frivolous delight called *In Praise of Baldness*. He designed a celestial map and invented a hydroscope with a weighted float to measure the specific gravity of liquids.

**Thomas à Kempis** (1379/80–1471)   German theologian and spiritual writer. Thomas is usually credited with the authorship of the *Imitation of Christ*, one of the most widely read Christian devotional books. A prolific writer, Thomas also wrote many other popular treatises on the life of the soul as well as lives of saints and religious conferences for monks. Some of his more famous works are the *Soliloquium animae* [Soliloquy of the Soul], which deals with the movement of grace, *De tribus tabernaculis*

[On the Three Tabernacles], reflections on poverty, humility, and chastity, *De fideli dispensatore* [On the Faithful Dispenser], which offers advice to a contemplative in charge of the material goods of the monastery, and *Sermones ad novicios*, thirty conferences for the Augustinian novices at Mount Saint Agnes in the Netherlands concerned with communal life, devotion to the Virgin Mary, and custody of the senses.

**Tyconius** (Fourth century A.D.)    Donatist writer of north Africa. A moderate Donatist who lived during the reign of the emperor Theodosius (378–395 A.D.), Tyconius wrote a commentary on the Apocalypse and a treatise entitled *De septem regulis* [On the Seven Rules], in which he lays down seven rules for discovering the true meaning of the Scriptures. His Donatism was flexible enough to admit the possibility of a church outside of his own sect.

**Ubertino of Casale** (c. 1259–c. 1330)    Theologian, preacher, and Franciscan Spiritual. As a young man, Ubertino of Casale was moved and influenced by the mystic Angela of Foligno, by John of Parma, who filled him with the apocalyptic visions of Joachim of Calabria, and by Pierre Olieu, the intellectual and charismatic center of the Spiritual movement. In 1304/5, Ubertino wrote his famous *Arbor vitae crucifixae Jesu* [The Tree of the Crucified Life of Jesus], a prose epic on the life and passion of Christ, followed by a commentary on the Apocalypse. Besides rapturous meditations on Saint Francis and evangelical poverty, the work contains vicious attacks on the laxity of the clergy and, especially, of the Franciscan order.

In the beginning Pope John XXII treated Ubertino almost with deference. When Ubertino refused to be reconciled to the Franciscans, John transferred him to the Benedictines. Eventually, however, their relationship disintegrated. In 1325, Ubertino was forced to flee from Avignon. Except for a sermon delivered in 1329 against John XXII, Ubertino's final years are shrouded in mystery.

**Ultima Thule**     A large island in the Northern Ocean (North Atlantic), a six days' journey from the Orkneys, believed by the ancients to be the northernmost boundary of the world. The soil of Ultima Thule was infertile; its air, a mixture of sea water and oxygen. Among the island's inhabitants were a friendly tribe famous for its excellent hydromel, or mead, a tribe that engaged in human sacrifice, and the Scritifines, a race of naked, barefooted teetotalers whose babies were given the marrow of wild animals to suck on rather than milk.

**Umiliati**     Members of a lay poverty movement, the Umiliati (Humiliati) were also called Berettini because of their ashen garments of undyed (*berretine, humile*) wool. They arose in Lombardy in the second half of the twelfth century. The Umiliati lived either as devout laity in the married state or in segregated convents observing religious chastity. Their desire to imitate the primitive Christians took the form of penitential austerity, frequent fasting, and personal and communal poverty. Manual laborers rather than mendicants, the men worked in the wool industry, while the women nursed the sick, especially lepers. Forbidden in 1179 by Pope Alexander III to preach in public, excommunicated in 1184 with the Waldensians by Pope Lucius III, the Umiliati were reinstated and reorganized by Pope Innocent III in 1201.

**Vallet, Claude Benjamin (Abbé)** (1754–1828)     French priest, historian, and politician. Abbé Vallet was the deputy from Gien from 1788 to 1807, first, to the Estates General and, then, to the National Assembly. In 1789, the deputies of the Third Estate, with the support of some clergy and aristocracy, converted the Estates General into a National Assembly. In 1790, Vallet wrote a history of the transactions of the *Salle de l'ordre du clergé* from the beginnings of the Estates General to its dissolution.

**Vincent Bel(l)ovacensis** (Died c. 1264)     French Dominican, medieval encyclopedist. Vincent Belovacensis, or Vincent of Beauvais, compiled an enormous encyclopedia entitled the *Speculum maius* [Greater Mirror], which was intended to reflect all knowledge. The work was divided into four parts—the mirrors of nature, doctrine, morality (which was not written by Vincent), and history. Vincent quotes from many Latin, Greek, Arabic, and Hebrew authors, including Plato, Aristotle, the *Physiologus*, Isidore of Seville, Rhazes, and Adelard of Bath. Too often, however, the *Speculum maius* is a tedious catalogue of popular superstitions and unsubstantiated opinions. For example, Vincent states that barnacle birds feed on driftwood until they reach maturity, agate wards off venomous animals, and coral, suspended from the neck, prevents epileptic seizures. Vincent also wrote a treatise *On the Education of Royal Children* and a consolatory tract addressed to King Louis IX of France when the latter had lost one of his children.

**Virgil of Toulouse** (Seventh century)    Grammarian. Virgil of Toulouse, also known as Vergilius Maro the Grammarian, is one of the most mysterious and eccentric figures in medieval Latin literature. With arrogant abandon, he assumed the name of Rome's greatest poet to hide his own identity and gave names such as Catullus, Cicero, and Aeneas to his teachers and friends. Virgil's two extant works are twelve *Epitomae*, short treatises on grammar, and eight *Letters* addressed to a deacon named Julius Germanus. Both works contain preposterous grammatical explanations, delightfully absurd etymologies, and ridiculous neologisms. Virgil argued that Latin nouns could be divided into four distinct genders. By separating and rearranging different verbal elements, he invented a secret language intelligible only to Virgil and his friends. Whether Virgil intended all of this as an elaborate parody of grammatical treatises or was moved by a kind of perverse intellectual earnestness in an era of cultural decline is still a mystery. In Ireland, however, he was taken quite seriously.

**Vitalis, Saint** (Third century A.D.)    Vitalis was the slave of Agricola of Bologna, from whom he learned the Christian faith.

During the reign of the emperor Diocletian (284–305 A.D.), Vitalis was put to death in the amphitheater. Agricola, inspired by his slave's example, put aside his fears and eagerly embraced the crown of martyrdom. He was placed on a cross, and nails were driven through his body. In 393, Eusebius, Bishop of Bologna, was told in a vision that the remains of Vitalis and Agricola lay in that city's Jewish cemetery. Their bodies were retrieved and venerated.

**Waldensians**  A religious movement founded by Valdes of Lyons, a rich merchant who abandoned his possessions in 1173 and began to preach. Valdes and his followers travelled to Rome in 1179, where Pope Alexander II approved their vow of poverty but warned them that laymen were forbidden to preach without permission. Before long, the Waldensians were regarded by many as dangerously anticlerical. At Verona in 1184, Pope Lucius III denounced the Waldensians, who were also called the Poor of Lyons, as heretics. The Umiliati, a contemporary lay movement among the wool workers of Milan, were likewise condemned at Verona. The members of the Umiliati joined the Waldensians to create a new sect called the Poor Lombards. The two groups soon realized that living together was hopeless, and in 1205 they separated.

**William of Moerbeke** (c. 1215–1286)  Belgian Dominican, archbishop, translator. A member of the Dominican community of Ghent, William of Moerbeke was a famous translator of Greek works. At Viterbo and Orvieto, he became a close friend of Thomas Aquinas, who asked him to translate several works for him. William was the personal advisor of Pope Gregory X and took part in the Council of Lyons in 1274. Finally, Pope Nicholas III appointed William archbishop of Corinth, where he lived until his death.

**Williamites**  The name of three religious orders and three heretical sects, none of which exists today. Eco is probably re-

ferring to the secret sect of men and women founded by
Wilhelmina of Milan, who claimed to be the incarnation of the
Holy Spirit. The sect was discovered and dissolved shortly after
her death in 1282.

Another heretical sect, also called the Williamites, was
founded by Aegidius Cantoris, a Belgian who called himself the
"Savior of Men." A Carmelite priest named William of
Hildernisse was accused of supporting the sect, and, for this
reason, his followers were called Williamites. Since these Williamites date to the late fourteenth century, they are too late to
be Eco's Williamites in *The Name of the Rose*.

# CHAPTER FOUR

# Notes on the Text of
# *The Name of the Rose*

*Including translations of all non-English passages*
In the lefthand column, all page and line numbers from the Harcourt Brace & Company clothbound (1983) and paperbound Harvest (1994) editions of *The Name of the Rose* appear in roman type, and all page and line numbers from the 1984 Warner Books paperbound edition appear in *italic type*.

## INTRODUCTION

| | |
|---|---|
| 1.2–4 | *Text* Abbé* Vallet, *Le Manuscrit de Dom* |
| *xiii.2–4* | *Adson de Melk, traduit en français d'après l'édition Dom J. Mabillon* (Aux Presses de l'Abbaye de la Source, Paris, 1842). |
| | *Trans.* Abbé* Vallet, *The Manuscript of Dom* Adso of Melk, translated into French and based on the edition of J. Mabillon* (The Presses of the Abbey of the Source, Paris, 1842). |
| | **Abbé* priest or abbot |
| | **Dom* A Benedictine title, short for *Dominus* (lord) |
| 2.15–26 | *Text Vetera analecta*, sive *collectio veterum,* |
| *xiv. 25–37* | et seq. |

*Trans.* *An Ancient Compilation*, or *A Collection of Several Ancient Works* and shorter works of every type, poems, letters, documents, epitaphs, and with *The German Itinerary* with explanations and comments by Reverend Father Dom Jean Mabillon, Priest and Monk of the Order of Saint Benedict and from the Congregation of Saint Maur (new edition); to which have been added a *Life of Mabillon* and a few shorter works, namely his *Discussion on the Eucharistic Bread, Unleavened and Leavened* for His Most Eminent Cardinal Bona. Attached is a short work by the Spanish Bishop Eldefonsus on the same subject, and the Letter of the Roman Eusebius to Theophilus of Gaul, *On the Cult of the Unknown Saints*. Paris, Levesque, near the Bridge of Saint Michael, 1721 (with the King's permission).

*Note* This is, in fact, an accurate listing of some of the principal works of **Jean Mabillon.** (See "Annotated Guide.")

2.31–32
*xv.4–5*

*Text* "Montalant, ad Ripam P.P. Augustinianorum (prope Pontem S. Michaelis)"

*Trans.* "Montalant, near the Bank of the Augustinian Fathers (beside the Bridge of Saint Michael)"

3.13–14
*xv.30–32*

*Text* ("en me retraçant ces détails, j'en suis

à me demander s'ils sont réels, ou bien si je les ai rêvés")

*Trans.* ("on going over these details, I've reached the point of wondering whether they're real or if I dreamed them")

4.38–39
*xvii.35–37*

*Text* [1]*Liber aggregationis seu liber secretorum Alberti Magni*, Londinium, juxta pontem qui vulgariter dicitur Flete brigge, MCCCC-LXXXV.

*Trans.* '*The Book of Accumulated Thoughts* or *The Book of Secrets of Albert the Great*, London (beside the Bridge commonly known as the Fleet Bridge), 1485.

5.1
*xviii.2*

*Text* the *Grand* and the *Petit Albert*

*Trans.* the *Great* and the *Little Albert*

5.36–39
*xviii.34–38*

*Text* [2]*Les Admirables Secrets d'Albert le Grand*, A Lyon, Chez les Héritiers Beringos, Fratres, à l'Enseigne d'Agrippa, MDCC-LXXV; *Secrets merveilleux de la magie naturelle et cabalistique du Petit Albert*, A Lyon, Chez les Héritiers Beringos, Fratres, à l'Enseigne d'Agrippa, MDCCXXIX.

*Trans.* [2]*The Admirable Secrets of Albert the Great*, Lyons (House of the Beringos Heirs, Brothers, at the Sign of Agrippa), 1775; *The Marvelous Secrets of the Natural and Cabalistic*

*Magic of the Little Albert,* Lyons (House of the Beringos Heirs, Brothers, at the Sign of Agrippa), 1729.

5.12–13
*xviii.16*

*Text* "Parbleu!" and "La femme, ah! la femme!"

*Trans.* "Good Lord, yes!" and "(The) woman, ah! (the) woman!"

5.31–32
*xix.6–7*

*Text* "In omnibus requiem quaesivi, et nusquam inveni nisi in angulo cum libro."

*Trans.* "I have sought tranquility in everything, but found it nowhere except in a corner with a book."

*Note* The words *In omnibus requiem quaesivi* are found in Ecclesiasticus 24:7 and were often quoted not only by **Thomas à Kempis,** but also by **Meister Eckhart** (See "Annotated Guide"). That **Thomas à Kempis** was fond of this saying is indicated by a contemporary portrait of him which shows the elderly writer in his study beside a book open to these words. A 1471 copy of the portrait still survives.

# NOTE

7.15–8.9    *Text*                          *Translation*
*xx.18–xxi.14*  *Les Heures bénédictines*    *The Benedictine Hours*

| | |
|---|---|
| Matins (or Matutini) | Morning Services or *Vigiliae* (Services of the Night Watch) |
| Lauds | Services of Praise, Short for *Laudate* (Praise!) |
| Prime | Services of the First Hour |
| Terce | Services of the Third Hour |
| Sext | Services of the Sixth Hour |
| Nones | Services of the Ninth Hour |
| Vespers | Evening Services |
| Compline | Services at the Completion of the Day (an alternative of *Completorium*) |

# PROLOGUE

12.21

*4.34*

*Text* Caput Mundi

*Trans.* Capital (literally, "Head") of the World

*Note* The expression "caput mundi" appears in several collections of poems of the eleventh to thirteenth centuries, particularly the *Carmina Burana* and the Cambridge Songs. *Carmina Burana* 19.4 is a satirical description of Rome as the *caput mundi* and makes many puns on both words—a proof of the popularity of the phrase.

13.11
*5.32*

***Text*** usus facti

***Trans.*** his to use (literally, "use in fact")

***Note*** In his bull of 1279 (*Exiit qui seminat*, cf. Eco 341/*411*), Nicholas III makes a distinction between *usus facti*, the use in fact of necessary things, and *usus iuris*, the right of use or possession. This is crucial to the question of Franciscan poverty and is dealt with at greater length by Eco on 335/*403* ff.

13.18
*6.2–3*

***Text*** *Cum inter nonnullos*

***Trans.*** *Since among several (learned men)*

***Note*** Titles of papal bulls are simply the first two or three words of the text. This bull begins "Cum inter nonnullos scholasticos viros . . ." (Since among several learned men . . .). The main thrust of the bull is a declaration that those who uphold the poverty of Christ (specifically the Franciscans of the Perugia chapter) are heretics. Eco discusses this further on 339/*408*.

17.25
*11.14*

***Text*** unico homine regente

***Trans.*** with only one man in control

17.28
*11.18*

> ***Text*** ad modum avis volantis
>
> ***Trans.*** in the manner of a bird flying

# FIRST DAY
Sunday, the first day of Advent

## PRIME

21.9
*15.11*

> ***Text*** Aedificium
>
> ***Trans.*** Huge Building

23.9
*17.30*

> ***Text*** Brunellus
>
> ***Trans.*** Browny

23.37–39
*18.28–30*

> ***Text*** *omnis mundi creatura*
> *quasi liber et pictura*
> *nobis est in speculum*
>
> ***Trans.*** Every creature of the world,
> like a picture and a book,
> appears to us as a mirror.
>
> ***Note*** It is a faithful sign, Alanus goes on to say, of our life. Interestingly, the next stanza continues: "The rose depicts our station, a fitting explanation of our lot, a reading of our life, which while it blooms in early morning, 'flowers out,' the flower

deflowered (*defloratus flos effloret*)." See Eco
279.1–5/*333.22–27*.

24.25
*19.24*

    ***Text*** siccum prope pelle ossibus adhaerente

    ***Trans.*** firm, with the skin closely outlining the bones

    ***Note*** This description of the horse is from **Isidore of Seville's** *Etymologies* or *Origins* 12.1.46. See "Annotated Guide" under **Isidore of Seville.**

24.31
*19.32*

    ***Text*** auctoritates

    ***Trans.*** authorities

    ***Note*** Eco repeats this often.

25.38
*21.11*

    ***Text*** balneary

    ***Trans.*** bathhouse

27.23–28.1
*24.8*

    ***Text*** verbum mentis

    ***Trans.*** universal concept (literally, "word of the mind")

    ***Note*** The term "verbum mentis" was used by **Thomas Aquinas** for the conceptual sign formed by the mind itself, the concept abstracted by the mind from the individual object of perception—a mental sign.

28.15
24.26

*Text* Niger

*Trans.* Black

33.22
31.8

*Text* scriptorium

*Trans.* writing room

*Note* The system of a scriptorium, or "writing room," and a library for the preservation of texts was first introduced by Cassiodorus at Vivarium, his monastery in Calabria. It became one of the distinctive features of the Benedictine monasteries, where writing in the scriptorium was the task of the most intelligent and, often, most ambitious monks. The scriptorium was ordinarily located near the kitchen or the calefactory, a heated room in which monks were allowed to warm themselves.

34.16–17
32.7–8

*Text* "Eris sacerdos in aeternum."

*Trans.* "You will be a priest forever."

*Note* "Thou art a priest forever after the order of Melchizedek." (Psalm 110; Hebrews 7:17).

34.35
32.30

*Text* coram monachis

*Trans.* in the monks' presence

36.5–8
*34.9–12*

*Text* "Monasterium sine libris . . . est sicut civitas sine opibus, castrum sine numeris, coquina sine suppellectili, mensa sine cibis, hortus sine herbis, pratum sine floribus, arbor sine foliis. . . .

*Trans.* "A monastery without books . . . is like a city without wealth, a fortress without troops, a kitchen without utensils, a table without food, **a** garden without plants, a meadow without flowers, a tree without leaves. . . ."

*Note* The author of these words is Jakob Louber, of the Carthusian monastery of Basel.

36.28
*34.38*

*Text* Mundus senescit.

*Trans.* The world is growing old.

*Note* See Eco 11.11/*3.13*.

*SEXT*

46.19–26
*47.9–18*

*Text* "Penitenziagite! Watch out for the draco, et seq.

*Trans.* "Repent! Watch out for the dragon who cometh in future to gnaw your soul! Death is upon us! Pray the Holy Father

come to free us from evil and all our sin!
Ha, ha, you like this black magic of our
Lord Jesus Christ! To me as well joy is pain,
and pleasure painful . . . Beware the devil!
Always lying in wait for me in some corner
to snap at my heels. But Salvatore is not
stupid! Good is the monastery, and the
dining-hall here and pray to our Lord. And
the rest is not worth shit. Amen. No?"

*Note* This is the first of Salvatore's babeliza-
tions. Wherever he appears, his speech is a
confusing amalgam of vulgar Latin, Proven-
çal, Italian, and Spanish/Catalan.

47.7
48.5

*Text* ad placitum

*Trans.* by agreement

47.17
48.17

*Text* disiecta membra

*Trans.* scattered fragments

*Note* See Eco 11.6–7/3.6–8

47.24–25
48.27

*Text* (si licet magnis componere parva . . .)

*Trans.* (if I may compare small things with
great . . .)

*Note* From Virgil, *Georgics* 4.176. The great
Roman poet Virgil, most famous for the
*Aeneid*, is, in the *Georgics*, instructing Ro-

mans in the art of husbandry. Book IV of the *Georgics* deals with beekeeping, and here Virgil is comparing the industry of Attic bees to that of the Cyclopes at the forge.

47.34–35
*49.1–3*

*Text* "Domine frate magnificentissimo, . . . Jesus venturus est and les hommes must do penitenzia. No?"

*Trans.* "My lord brother most magnificent, . . . Jesus is about to come and men must do penitence. No?"

47.39
*49.6*

*Text* "Non comprends."

*Trans.* "I don't understand."

48.4–5
*49.12*

*Text* "vade retro"

*Trans.* "get thee behind me"

*Note* From Mark 8:31–33: "And [Jesus] began to teach them, that the Son of man must suffer many things, and be rejected of the elders, and of the chief priests, and scribes, and be killed, and after three days rise again. And he spake that saying openly. And Peter took him, and began to rebuke him. But when he had turned about and looked on his disciples, he rebuked Peter, saying, Get thee behind me, Satan: for thou savourest not the things that be of God, but the things that be of men."

This is reminiscent of Matthew 4, where Jesus is led up into the wilderness and tempted by the devil three times. Finally Jesus says, "Get thee hence, Satan (*vade, Satanas*): for it is written, Thou shalt worship the Lord thy God, and him only shalt thou serve."

49.3
*50.20*

**Text** *Arbor vitae crucifixae.*

**Trans.** *The Tree of the Crucified Life.*

**Note** In *Paradiso* XII, Dante has **Bonaventure** criticize **Ubertino** for his excessive strictness in observing the Franciscan rule. See "Annotated Guide" under **Bonaventure of Bagnoregio.** See Eco 53.5/*55.27.*

51.19–20
*53.24–25*

**Text** fratres et pauperes heremitae domini Celestini

**Trans.** brothers and poor hermits of Dom Celestine

52.9
*54.20*

**Text** *Firma cautela*

**Trans.** *With Firm Precaution*

**Note** This bull of Boniface VIII was issued in 1296.

53.17
*56.3–4*

**Text** *Exivi de paradiso*

***Trans.*** *I have left Paradise*

***Note*** This bull, one of the fruits of the Council of Vienne (in session from October 1311 to May 1312), was issued by Pope Clement V on May 6, 1312. It began by affirming the three vows of the Franciscan rule—chastity, poverty, and obedience. It discussed the handling of such matters as clothing, shoes, preaching, fasting, etc. It enjoined the Franciscans not to accept in alms more than they needed and listed abuses against the spirit of poverty, i.e. large holdings in buildings, rich furnishings, etc. It ended, however, with the demand that the warring parties within the Franciscan order live in peace together and that neither party—the Spirituals who upheld the strictest interpretation of poverty or the Conventuals who embraced a more relaxed position—call the other heretics.

54.1–2
*56.30–31*

***Text*** per mundum discurrit vagabundus

***Trans.*** travelled throughout the world as a vagabond

55.38
*59.7–8*

***Text*** *Ad conditorem canonum*

***Trans.*** *To the Founder of the Rules*

***Note*** This bull, issued by **John XXII** on December 8, 1322, was in direct opposition to the Franciscan chapter at Perugia. John rejects simple *usus facti* (use in fact) and gives to the Franciscans, against their will, possession of the things they used. (Eco refers to this bull again on 339/*408*.)

57.18–19
*60.38*

**Text** Spiritus Libertatis

**Trans.** Spirit of Freedom

57.28–30
*61.12–14*

**Text** homo nudus cum nuda iacebat . . . et non commiscebantur ad invicem

**Trans.** a naked man lay with a naked woman . . . but they did not couple with one another

61.28
*66.9–10*

**Text** lignum vitae

**Trans.** tree (literally, "wood") of life

62.37–63.1
*67.31–34*

**Text** "Quorum primus seraphico calculo purgatus et ardore celico inflammatus totum incendere videbatur. Secundus vero verbo predicationis fecundus super mundi tenebras clarius radiavit. . . ."

**Trans.** "The first of whom, purified by seraphic coal and inflamed with heavenly inspiration, appeared to set the entire world on fire. The second, bursting with the true word of prophecy, shone brightly above the darkness of the world. . . ."

64.28–29
70.2–3

**Text** Mors est quies viatoris—finis est omnis laboris.

**Trans.** Death is the traveller's rest—the end of all his labor.

## TOWARD NONES

67.20–34
74.5–21

| **Text** | **Translation** |
|---|---|
| Theatrum Sanitatis | Treatise (literally, "Theater of") on Health |
| De virtutibus herbarum | On the Beneficial Qualities of Herbs |
| De plantis | On Plants |
| De vegetalibus | On Vegetables (literally, "vegetal substances") |
| De causis | On Causes |

68.4
74.30

**Text** lectio divina

**Trans.** sacred reading (private reading of the Holy Scripture)

## AFTER NONES

75.5–10
83.7–13

**Text** "De pentagono Salomonis, Ars loquendi, et seq.

**Trans.** "On the Pentagon of Solomon, The Art of Speaking and Understanding the Hebrew Language, On the Properties of Metals by Roger of Hereford, Algebra by Al-Kuwarizmi, translated into Latin by Robert the Englishman, the *Punic Wars* of Silius Italicus, *The Deeds of the Franks* (*French*), *On the Celebration of the Holy Cross* by Rabanus Maurus, and *Flavius Claudius Giordanus' On the Age of the World and Man* (arranged in books alphabetically from A to Z)"

75.18–24
*83.22–29*

*Text* "iii, IV gradus, V in prima graecorum"; "ii, V gradus, VII in tertia anglorum"

*Trans.* "third book, fourth shelf, fifth case in the first of the Greeks"; "second book, fifth shelf, seventh case in the third of the English (Angles)"

76.35
*85.15*

*Text* in aenigmate

*Trans.* darkly

*Note* See Note 80.23/*89.33*.

77.21
*86.6*

*Text* "verba"

*Trans.* "words"

77.35–36
*86.23*

*Text* "Sanctus, Sanctus, Sanctus"

*Trans.* "Holy, Holy, Holy"

*Note* This is from the Canon of the Mass: "Holy, Holy, Holy, Lord God of Hosts.

Heaven and earth are full of Your glory. Hosanna in the highest! (Isaiah 6:3) Blessed is He who comes in the name of the Lord. Hosanna in the highest! (Matthew 21:9)." The triple form was intended as an affirmation of the Trinity.

78.17–19
*87.9–11*

*Text Aller wunder si geswigen,
das erde himel hât überstigen,
daz sult ir vür ein wunder wigen.*

***Trans.*** Be silent about all wonders;
That earth has risen above heaven—
This you should consider a wonder.

78.23–25
*87.15–17*

*Text Erd ob un himel unter,
das sult ir hân besunder
vür aller wunder ein wunder.*

***Trans.*** Earth above, heaven under,
This, above all, consider
To be wonder of wonders.

78.39
*87.33*

*Text* "Verba vana aut risui apta non loqui."

***Trans.*** "Speak not words which are idle or suitable for laughter."

***Note*** From the Benedictine Rule, Chapter 4, "Quae sunt instrumenta bonorum," "These are the tools of good works."

79.33
88.36

*Text* exempla

*Trans.* examples


80.23
89.33

*Text* per speculum et in aenigmate

*Trans.* in a mirror and obscurely

*Note* See Saint Paul, I Corinthians 13:12.
". . . through a glass darkly."


83.12
93.14–15

*Text Libellus de Antichristo*

*Trans. Short Book on the Antichrist*


*VESPERS*


86.23
97.10–11

*Text* "Oculi de vitro cum capsula!"

*Trans.* "Eyeglasses (literally, "eyes of glass") with a frame!"


86.29–30
97.18

*Text* ab oculis ad legendum

*Trans.* for (literally, "from") the eyes for reading

*Note* Venetian documents from the fourteenth century mention *vitreos ab oculis ad legendum* and *oculos de vitro cum capsula*. The earliest spectacles were for far-sighted people, since that type of lens was easier to manufacture.

87.19
*98.13*

**Text** tamquam ab iniustis possessoribus

**Trans.** as if from unworthy owners

*COMPLINE*

93.17–18
*106.1–2*

**Text** "Benedicite" . . . "Edent pauperes."

**Trans.** "Bless the Lord" . . . "The poor will eat."

**Note** From Psalm 22:26. This was used as a grace before meals in Benedictine as well as other religious communities.

95.32
*108.20*

**Text** "Manduca, iam coctum est"

**Trans.** "Eat, it is already cooked"

95.38
*108.27*

**Text** *Peristephanon*

**Trans.** (*Book*) *of Crowns*

**Note** See "Annotated Guide" under **Prudentius.**

96.33–36
*109.29–32*

**Text** "Tu autem Domine miserere nobis."

"Adiutorium nostrum in nomine Domini . . .
Qui fecit coelum et terram."

*Trans.* "But You, O Lord, have mercy
on us . . . Our help is in the name of the
Lord . . . Who made heaven and earth."

*Note* These words are taken from the
prayers at the foot of the altar at the beginning of the Mass.

# SECOND DAY
Monday

*MATINS*

101.15–16
*114.1–2*

*Text* "Benedicamus Domino . . . Deo
gratias."

*Trans.* "Let us bless the Lord . . . Thanks
be to God."

*Note* In the early hours of the morning, the
monks were awakened with the words
"Benedicamus Domino." The appropriate
response was "Deo gratias."

101.22
*114.9–10*

*Text* "Domine labia mea aperies et os
meum annuntiabit laudem tuam."

*Trans.* "O Lord, open my lips and my

mouth shall proclaim Thy praise." (Psalm 51:15)

102.2
*114.13*

**Text** "Venite exultemus"

**Trans.** "Come let us rejoice" (Psalm 95:1)

102.24
*115.3*

**Text** "Te Deum (laudamus)"

**Trans.** "Thee, O God, (we praise)"

**Note** This hymn, formerly attributed to Saint Ambrose, was probably written at the end of the fourth or the beginning of the fifth century by the Rumanian bishop Nicetas.

103.17–18
*116.4–5*

**Text.** "Deus qui est sanctorum splendor mirabilis" and "Iam lucis orto sidere."

**Trans.** "God who is the wondrous splendor of the saints" and "Already the star of light has risen."

**Note** The second hymn is in the *Carmina Burana* (119), and is at least as old as the fifth century.

106.38
*120.19*

**Text** "Omnis mundi creatura, quasi liber et scriptura . . ."

*Trans.* "Every creature of the world, Like a scripture and a book . . ."

*Note* Here Adso replaces the original "pictura" of **Alanus de Insulis** with "scriptura". See Eco 23.37–39/*18.28–30.*

107.7
*120.27*

*Text* 'Credo in unum Deum.'

*Trans.* 'I believe in one God.'

*Note* The Nicene Creed begins with these words and is used as the declaration of faith in the Mass.

## PRIME

111.26–27
*126.1*

*Text* infima doctrina

*Trans.* the lowest form of instruction

111.36
*126.12*

*Text* naturaliter

*Trans.* naturally

*Note* A person could be considered "naturaliter" Christian if his works showed a Christian spirit even without benefit of baptism or revelation.

112.33–35
*127.15–17*

*Text* Est domus in terris, *clara quae voce resultat.*

*Ipsa domus resonat, tacitus sed non sonat hospes.*
*Ambo tamen currunt, hospes simul et domus una.*

**Trans.** There is a house on the earth which rings with a clear tone.
The house itself resounds, but the silent guest makes no sound.
Yet both hurry on, the guest and the house together.

*Note* The riddles of **Symphosius** were probably composed in the fourth or fifth century. (See "Annotated Guide") In this riddle, the house is a river and its guest, or inhabitant, is a fish. In contrast to most houses, this house makes noise while its guest is silent. Yet both flow together (note the play on the word "currunt"), the river and the fish.

113.35
*128.26*

*Text* 'finis Africae'

**Trans.** 'the end of Africa'

*Note* This expression occurs about thirty times in the novel.

120.8–11
*136.18–21*

*Text* speculum mundi

**Trans.** mirror of the world

*TERCE*

121.13–14
*137.16–18*

*Text* "Filii Dei they are, et seq.

*Trans.* "Sons of God they are, . . . Jesus has said that you do for him what you do for one of these children!"

121.19–20
*138.5–6*

*Text* "I am a monk Sancti Benedicti! Merdre à toy, Bogomil de merdre!"

*Trans.* "I am a monk of Saint Benedict! Shit on you, Bogomil of shit!"

122.2–4
*138.12–13*

*Text* ". . . tell him the filii de Francesco non sunt hereticos!" . . . "Ille menteur, puah!"

*Trans.* ". . . tell him the sons of Francis are not heretics!" . . . "That liar, puah!"

130.22–24
*149.2–3*

*Text* 'fabulas poetae a *fando* nominaverunt, quia non sunt *res factae* sed tantum loquendo *fictae*. . . .'

*Trans.* 'Poets have named them fables from speaking (*fando*), because they are not facts (*factae*) but only fictions, the creations (*fictae*) of speech. . . .'

*Note* From **Isidore of Seville,** *Etymologies* 1.40.1. See "Annotated Guide."

131.18
*150.5*

*Text* stultus in risu exaltat vocem suam.

*Trans.* A fool exalts his voice in laughter.

*Note* From *Rule of Saint Benedict*, Chapter 7, "De humilitate", "On Humility".

131.24–26
*150.12–15*

*Text* 'Scurrilitates vero vel verba otiosa et risum moventia aeterna clausura in omnibus locis damnamus, et ad talia eloquia discipulum aperire os non permittitur.'

*Trans.* 'But buffoonery or words which are useless and provoke laughter—these we condemn on all occasions with a perpetual ban, and the disciple is not permitted to open his mouth for such conversation.'

*Note* From *Rule of Saint Benedict*, Chapter 6, "De taciturnitate", "On Silence."
This same passage was part of the sacred reading at the evening meal on the First Day (95/*108*): "But vulgarities, nonsense, and jests we condemn to perpetual imprisonment, in every place, and we do not allow the disciple to open his mouth for speech of this sort."

131.37
*150.28–29*

*Text* spiritualiter salsa

*Trans.* spiritually pointed (witty)

132.1–2
*150.32*

*Text De habitu et conversatione monachorum*

**Trans.** *On the Dress and Conversation of Monks*

132.4–5
*150.35–36*

**Text** 'Admittenda tibi ioca sunt post seria quaedam, sed tamen et dignis et ipsa gerenda modis.'

**Trans.** 'After some serious discussions, you ought to allow jokes; but still these must be governed by suitable restraints.'

132.25
*151.21–22*

**Text** 'Deus non est.'

**Trans.** 'There is no God.'

133.24
*152.31*

**Text** 'Tu es petrus.'

**Trans.** 'You are the rock.'

**Note** From Matthew 16:18. Jesus asks his disciples who the Son of Man is and Simon Peter responds, " 'Thou art the Christ, the Son of the living God.' And Jesus answered and said unto him, 'Blessed art thou, Simon Barjonah: for flesh and blood hath not revealed it unto thee, but my Father which is in heaven. And I say also unto thee, That thou art Peter, and upon this rock I will build my church; and the gates of hell shall not prevail against it.' "

There is a pun on the meaning of the name "Peter," in Greek, "rock, stone."

133.30
*152.38*

    *Text Speculum stultorum*

    *Trans.* *Mirror of Fools*

    *Note* See "Annotated Guide."

133.37–38
*153.10*

    *Text* Tum podex carmen extulit horridulum.

    *Trans.* Then his asshole let out a vulgar sound.

*NONES*

146.17–18
*167.21*

    *Text* ordo monachorum

    *Trans.* order of monks

150.34–35
*173.5–6*

    *Text* the Bogomil heresy of the ordo Bulgariae and the ordo Drygonthie

    *Trans.* the Bogomil heresy of the Bulgarian order and the Dragovitsan order

155.17
*178.30*

    *Text* "Salva me ab ore leonis"

    *Trans.* "Save me from the lion's mouth" (Psalm 22:21)

## AFTER VESPERS

158.1–2
*181.21–23*

*Text* "Hunc mundum tipice labyrinthus denotat ille . . . Intranti largus, redeunti sed nimis artus."

*Trans.* "The labyrinth represents the world allegorically . . . Spacious for the one entering, but extremely narrow for the one returning."

*Note* This inscription, dated 903 A.D., appears, together with the signs of the zodiac, in the church of San Savino in Piacenza. It goes on to say that he who is captivated by this world and weighed down by the burden of his vices is able to return only with difficulty to the doctrine of life.

158.9
*181.30*

*Text* ossarium

*Trans.* a bone-vault

159.24
*183.17*

*Text* aqua fons vitae

*Trans.* water, the source of life

## COMPLINE

163.10
*188.1*

*Text* "Mane, Tekel, Peres"

*Note* From Daniel 5:25–28. These three

words are the famous handwriting on the wall in the Book of Daniel. "Belshazzar the king made a great feast to a thousand of his lords. . . . In the same hour came forth fingers of a man's hand, and wrote over against the candlestick upon the plaster of the wall of the king's palace." (5:1,5). The king sends for astrologers to interpret the words on the wall, but they cannot. Eventually, Daniel is brought in to interpret. "This is the interpretation of the thing: Mene; God hath numbered thy kingdom, and finished it. Tekel; Thou art weighed in the balances, and art found wanting. Peres; Thy kingdom is divided, and given to the Medes and the Persians. . . . And in that night was Belshazzar the king of the Chaldeans slain." (5:25–28, 30).

166.27
*192.13*

*Text* 'Secretum finis Africae'

*Trans.* 'Secret of the end of Africa'

167.3
*192.32*

*Text* "Graecum est, non legitur"

*Trans.* "It is Greek, and not readable"

*NIGHT*

169.19
*196.5–6*

*Text* "Apocalypsis Iesu Christi."

*Trans.* "The Apocalypse of Jesus Christ."

*Note* See Eco 171.9,12/*197.31,35*.

170.8
*196.21*

*Text* "Super thronos viginti quatuor"

*Trans.* "On their thrones sat the twenty-four elders"

*Note* From Revelation 4:4. This and almost all of the following quotations in this chapter are taken from the Book of Revelation, also called the Apocalypse.

170.9
*196.22*

*Text* "Nomen illi mors."

*Trans.* "His name was death." (Revelation 6:8)

170.17–18
*196.33–34*

*Text* "Obscuratus est sol et aer"

*Trans.* "Sun and air were darkened" (Revelation 9:2)

170.19–20
*196.35–36*

*Text* "Facta est grando et ignis"

*Trans.* "There was hail and fire" (Revelation 8:7)

171.4
*197.26*

*Text* "In diebus illis"

*Trans.* "In those days" (Revelation 9:6)

171.7–8
*197.29–30*

*Text* "Primogenitus mortuorum"

*Trans.* "The firstborn of the dead" (Revelation 1:5)

171.13–14
*197.36–37*

*Text* "Cecidit de coelo stella magna"

*Trans.* "A great star fell from the heavens" (Revelation 8:10)

171.32–33
*198.21*

*Text* "Equus albus"

*Trans.* "A white horse" (Revelation 6:2)

171.36
*198.24–25*

*Text* "Gratia vobis et pax"

*Trans.* "Grace to you and peace" (Revelation 1:4)

172.2–3
*198.30–31*

*Text* "Tertia pars terrae combusta est."

*Trans.* "A third of the earth was burned up." (Revelation 8:7)

172.27
*199.22*

*Text* *De aspectibus*

*Trans.* *On Optics* (literally, "images")

173.2–3
*200.2*

*Text* oculi ad legendum

*Trans.* eyes for reading

*Note* See *Note* 86.29–30/97.18.

| | |
|---|---|
| 173.12<br>*200.13* | *Text Tabulae*<br><br>*Trans.* Tables |
| 173.15<br>*200.16* | *Text De oculis . . . De radiis stellatis*<br><br>*Trans.* On Eyes . . . On Rays from the Stars |
| 173.17<br>*200.18–19* | *Text De bestiis*<br><br>*Trans.* On Beasts |
| 173.22<br>*200.23* | *Text Liber monstrorum de diversis generibus*<br><br>*Trans.* Book of Monsters of Various Kinds |
| 175.16–17<br>*202.37–38* | *Text* "Requiescant a laboribus suis"<br><br>*Trans.* "May they rest from their labors" (Revelation 14:13) |
| 175.22–23<br>*203.7* | *Text* mulier amicta sole<br><br>*Trans.* a woman robed in the sun<br><br>*Note* From Revelation 12:1–5: "And there appeared a great wonder in heaven; a woman clothed with the sun, and the moon under |

her feet, and upon her head a crown of twelve stars: And she being with child cried, travailing in birth, and pained to be delivered. And there appeared another wonder in heaven; and behold a great red dragon, having seven heads and ten horns, and seven crowns upon his heads. . . . and the dragon stood before the woman which was ready to be delivered, for to devour her child as soon as it was born. And she brought forth a man child, who was to rule all nations with a rod of iron: and her child was caught up unto God, and to his throne."

Eco refers again to the *mulier* in his article "Waiting for the millennium" (*FMR*, p. 79): "The Apocalyptic allegory is fairly obvious: though the woman may be identified as Eve, or else as the chosen people into whose midst the Messiah is born, and by association, the Church, liturgical tradition establishes that she is Mary."

## THIRD DAY
Tuesday

*TERCE*

184.2–7
214.13–19

*Text Quinti Sereni de medicamentis, Phaenomena*, et seq.

*Trans.* Quintus Serenus' *Medicines*, (Aratus') *Phenomena*, Aesop's *Book on the Nature of Animals, Cosmography: A Book of Aethicus*

*Peronymus, On the Holy Places Overseas: Three Books* which the Bishop Arculf arranged to be written with Adamnan as his scribe, Quintus Julius Hilarius' *Small Book on the Origin of the World*, Solinus' *Polyhistor: On the World's Geography and its Marvels, Almagest . . .*

184.10
*214.23*

*Text* terra incognita

*Trans.* an unknown land

185.6–7
*215.29*

*Text* sic et non

*Trans.* yes and no

*Note* This is clearly a reference to Abelard's most famous work, the *Sic et Non* (See "Annotated Guide" under **Abelard, Peter.**) Eco himself mentions Abelard on 132/*151*, "who wanted to submit all problems to the cold, lifeless scrutiny of reason not enlightened by Scripture, pronouncing his It-is-so and It-is-not-so."

187.23
*219.10*

*Text* "homeni malissimi"

*Trans.* "very wicked men"

*NONES*

206.2–4
*242.12–13*

*Text* 'Quod enim laicali ruditate turgescit non habet effectum nisi fortuito'

*Trans.* 'For what grows from simple igno-rance has no effect except by chance'

206.4–6
*242.15–16*

*Text* 'Sed opera sapientiae certa lege val-lantur et in fine debitum efficaciter diriguntur.'

*Trans.* 'But the works of wisdom are pro-tected by a fixed law and are effectively directed towards a necessary end.'

208.31
*245.24*

*Text* 'unum' and 'velut'

*Trans.* 'one' and 'as'

209.1–2
*245.34–36*

*Text* "Secretum finis Africae, et seq.

*Trans.* "For the secret of the end of Africa, place the hands over the idol on the first and the seventh of the four." This is trans-lated in the text as "The hand over the idol works on the first and the seventh of the four."

*VESPERS*

210.17–18
*248.2–3*

*Text Practica officii inquisitionis heretice pra-vitatis*

*Trans. A Handbook on the Conduct of an In-quisition into Heretical Depravity*

214.29
*252.37*

*Text* 'hic lapis gerit in se similitudinem coeli'

*Trans.* 'This stone contains within itself a likeness of the heavens'

219.18–20
*258.30–33*

*Text* "No se puede. Abbonis est, et seq.

*Trans.* "It is not possible. It is Abo's. But you do not need a handsome horse to ride hard . . . That one also suffices . . . Look there, the third (of the) horse . . ."

*Note* Salvatore's Latin is again inaccurate. He has said "the third of the horse" instead of "the third horse."

220.3–8
*259.22–28*

*Text* "Facilis. You take the cheese before it is too antiquum, et seq.

*Trans.* "Easy. You take the cheese before it is too old, without too much salt, and cut in cubes or any way you like. And then you put a bit of butter or lard to warm over the embers. And in it you put two pieces of cheese, and when it becomes soft, sugar and cinnamon are to be put on twice. And immediately take to table, because it must be ate hot hot."

220.15–16
*259.36–38*

*Text* "Sais pas, moi, . . . Peut-être your magister wants to go in dark place esta noche."

*Trans.* "I don't know . . . Maybe your master wants to go in dark place tonight."

## AFTER COMPLINE

222.13–15
262.25–27

*Text* 'Penitenziagite!' which was the uneducated man's way of saying 'Penitentiam agite, appropinquabit enim regnum coelorum.'

*Trans.* 'Repent' which was the uneducated man's way of saying 'Do penance, for the kingdom of heaven is at hand.' (Matthew 3:2)

225.29
266.35

*Text* "De hoc satis"

*Trans.* "Enough about this"

232.11
275.4

*Text Historia fratris Dulcini Heresiarche.*

*Trans. History of Fra Dolcino, Heresiarch.*

235.21–23
279.5–8

*Text* "In nomine Domini amen. Hec est quedam, et seq.

*Trans.* "In the name of the Lord, amen. This is a condemnation of the body and a sentence of corporal condemnation: brought, imposed and, in this decree, briefly declared and made public . . ."

235.34–38
*279.20–24*

*Text* Idcirco, dictum Johannem vocatum fratrem, et seq.

*Trans.* For that reason, it is decreed that John (called Brother Michael), a heretic and a schismatic, be led to the usual place of justice, and in that very place be burned and consumed by kindled fire and glowing flames, so that he may perish utterly and his soul be separated from his body.

236.30–31
*280.24–25*

*Text* "Per Dominum moriemur."

*Trans.* "We will die through the Lord."

239.8
*283.31*

*Text* "Credo"

*Trans.* "I believe"

240.11
*285.4*

*Text* Ultima Thule

*Trans.* the Far North

*Note* See "Annotated Guide."

240.17
*285.11*

*Text* *Physiologus*

*Trans.* *The Naturalist*

*Note* See "Annotated Guide."

241.12
286.16

*Text* "De te fabula narratur"

*Trans.* "The story is about you"

*Note* These words are from the first book of *Satires* (1.1.69–70) of the Roman poet Horace (65–8 B.C.). He criticizes men here for their avarice, which is the cause of all their unhappiness. "Tantalus," Horace says, "reaches out thirstily for the river which retreats from his lips. You laugh? Only change the name and *the story is about you.*" Eco quotes this line again in his article "Waiting for the millennium," where he is speaking of the importance of the Apocalypse to the people of the tenth century. "The Apocalypse with its Horsemen seems, to the stunned populace, who hear it narrated by monks and parish priests, a chronicle of the present time. The opening of each seal must have appeared to a medieval listener much as the front page of the morning paper appears to us. *De te fabula narratur.*"

241.18,22
286.23,28

*Text* mulier amicta sole

*Trans.* a woman robed in the sun (See Eco 175/*203*)

242.39
288.*19–20*

*Text* "Vade retro!"

*Trans.* "Get thee behind me!" (See Eco 48/*49*)

243.2
*288.21*

*Text* vis appetitiva

*Trans.* natural desire (appetitive drive)


243.39
*289.29–30*

*Text* valde bona

*Trans.* exceedingly good

*Note* From Genesis 1:31: At the end of the sixth day, after the creation of man and woman, "God saw all that he had made, and it was very good (*valde bona*)."


245.21
*291.29*

*Text* terribilis ut castorum acies ordinata

*Trans.* terrible as the ordered ranks of the chaste.


245.32–33
*292.5–6*

*Text* "Pulchra sunt ubera quae paululum supereminent et tument modice"

*Trans.* "Beautiful are the breasts which protrude slightly, only faintly tumescent"

*Note* These lines are from Gilbert of Hoyt's *Sermons on the Song of Solomon* XXXI, 4. Gilbert digresses from his allegorical interpretation of the Song of Songs in order to pontificate on the most pleasing physical dimensions of female breasts. See **Ubertino**'s speech, Eco 230/*273*.

245.38–39
*292.12–14*

**Text** "O sidus clarum puellarum . . . o porta clausa, fons hortorum, cella custos unguentorum, cella pigmentaria!"

**Trans.** "O bright star of maidens . . . O closed gate, fountain of my gardens, guardian vessel of unguents, chamber of perfume!"

**Note** Adso quotes first from the Ripoll collection of anonymous poems (*o sidus clarum puellarum*). The rest is from Adam of St. Victor's sequence "Salve Mater Salvatoris," referring to the Mother of God.

246.6
*292.20–21*

**Text** "O langueo . . . Causam languoris video nec caveo!"

**Trans.** "O, I am faint . . . I see the reason for my weakness and I do not avoid it!"

**Note** This forms a refrain in a poem sometimes called the Poem of the British Museum (MS Arundel 384). The poet is describing the conflict which had him fluctuating between love on one side, reason on the other. (It also occurs in *Carmina Burana* 159.4).

246.14
*292.31*

**Text** cuncta erant bona.

**Trans.** everything was good.

**Note** From Genesis 1:31: *cuncta . . . erant valde bona*. See Eco 243/*289*.

250.5–6
*297.21*

**Text** Omne animal triste post coitum.

**Trans.** Every animal is sad after inter-course.

## FOURTH DAY
Wednesday

*LAUDS*

261.16–17
*311.38–312.1*

**Text** nihil sequitur geminis ex particular-ibus unquam.

**Trans.** Nothing ever follows from two par-ticulars.

261.22
*312.8–9*

**Text** aut semel aut iterum medium gener-aliter esto

**Trans.** either once or twice the middle term shall be general

261.29
*312.17*

**Text** Darii

**Note.** William refers here to one of the chief errors of logical reasoning, the fallacy of the Undistributed Middle. Like the mathemat-ical equations $A = B$, $B = C$, $\therefore$ $C = A$, every syllogism is composed of three propositions (two premises and a conclusion) involving three terms.

All pirates are thieves.
Some sailors are pirates.
Therefore some sailors are thieves.

In this syllogism, pirates is the "middle" term and, in the first proposition, it is distributed, or general, i.e. it applies to all members of a class: all pirates are thieves— there are no pirates who are not thieves.

When Severinus says, "Two dead men both with blackened fingers. What do you deduce from that?", William says, "I deduce nothing: *nihil sequitur geminis ex particularibus unquam* (nothing ever follows from two particulars)." For, although Venantius had blackened fingers and is dead and Berengar had blackened fingers and is dead, there may be other people, besides Venantius and Berengar, who have blackened fingers who are either dead or alive.

William then suggests a new major premise: "A substance exists that blackens fingers." This can be restated as: "Substance X blackens fingers." Adso continues the syllogism:

Substance X blackens fingers.

Venantius and Berengar have blackened fingers.

Therefore, Venantius and Berengar touched substance X.

But Adso's syllogism is still invalid; the middle term, blackened fingers, is undistributed (particular) in both premises. Other things might blacken fingers as well. *"Aut semel aut iterum medium generaliter esto* (Either once or twice the middle must be general)."

William then suggests a third syllogism. "All those and only those who have blackened fingers have certainly touched a given substance." This leads to the syllogism:

All blackened fingers come from substance X.

Venantius and Berengar have blackened fingers.

Therefore Venantius and Berengar touched substance X.

The middle term—blackened fingers—is general (distributed) in the major premise, and so William avoids the fallacy of the Undistributed Middle.

William now says that with this syllogism, we "have a Darii, an excellent third mode of the first syllogistic figure." Syllogisms, then, have figures and modes!

There are four figures of the syllogism, determined by the position in the two premises of the major (P), minor (S), and middle (M) terms:

|                | (1) | (2) | (3) | (4) |
|----------------|-----|-----|-----|-----|
| Major premise: | M-P | P-M | M-P | P-M |
| Minor premise: | S-M | S-M | M-S | M-S |

(1) All pirates (M) are thieves (P).
Some sailors (S) are pirates (M).
Some sailors are thieves.

(2) No tulips (P) have thorns (M).
All roses (S) have thorns (M).
No roses are tulips.

(3) Some poodles (M) are black (P).
All poodles (M) are dogs (S).
Some dogs are black.

(4) Some sailors (P) are pirates (M).
All pirates (M) are thieves (S).
Some thieves are sailors.

Each of these figures has, unfortunately, several modes, or moods, in which the propositions are identified by letters:

An "A" proposition is universal and positive: all dogs are living.

An "E" proposition is universal and negative: No dogs have horns.

An "I" proposition is particular and positive: Some dogs are large.

An "O" proposition is particular and negative: Some dogs are not small.

William's syllogism is a syllogism of the first figure: M-P, S-M, S-P. For syllogisms of this figure, four modes are possible:

A  All plants are living.
A  All trees are plants.
A  All trees are living.

E  No dogs have horns.
A  All cows have horns.
E  No cows are dogs.

A  All heroes are brave.
I  Some Greeks are heroes.
I  Some Greeks are brave.

E  No heroes are cowards.
I  Some politicians are heroes.
O  Some politicians are not cowards.

These modes were given names to make them easier to remember. For the first figure the four modes are called BArbArA, CElArEnt, DArII, and FErIO. And so William's syllogism is a Darii:

A    All blackened fingers come from substance X (M-P).

I    Some monks (Venantius and Berengar) have blackened fingers (S-M).

I    Some monks (Venantius and Berengar) have touched substance X (S-P).

Having followed William this far, Adso
says, "Then we have the answer!" William's
response is, "Alas, Adso, you have too much
faith in syllogisms!" The reasoning is accurate, the logic is perfect, but the major
premise is unproved and so the whole syllogism falls flat on its face. Adso's final ob-
servations only point out the labyrinthine
qualities of logic: "useful when you entered
it but then left it." (See Eco 158/*181* on the
labyrinth and 492/*600* on the ladder.)

## PRIME

267.32–33
*320.10–11*

*Text* "Oh, a female who sells herself like
mercandia cannot be bona or have cortesia"

*Trans.* "Oh, a female who sells herself like
merchandise cannot be good or have re-
spect"

267.36
*320.14–15*

*Text* "Deu, . . . They think dì e noche
about how to trap a man. . . ."

*Trans.* "God, . . . They think day and
night about how to trap a man. . . ."

269.37–38
*322.32–33*

*Text* "Ad mulieres pauperes in villulis"

*Trans.* "To Poor Women in Villages"

275.30
329.33

*Text* "Kyrie."

*Trans.* "Lord."

*Note* This is part of a prayer from the early part of the Mass, the only Greek remaining in the Latin Mass: Kyrie eleison, Christe eleison, Kyrie eleison (Lord, have mercy; Christ, have mercy; Lord, have mercy).

*TERCE*

280.24–25
335.22

*Text* amor est magis cognitivus quam cognitio

*Trans.* love is wiser than wisdom

280.27
335.26

*Text* intus et in cute

*Trans.* inside and out

281.14–15
336.21

*Text* motus in amatum

*Trans.* a feeling for the beloved

282.5–6
337.21

*Text* "agnus" . . . "agnoscit"

*Trans.* "lamb" . . . "recognizes"

*Note* From **Isidore of Seville,** *Etymologies* 12.1.12. See "Annotated Guide."

282.9
*337.26*

*Text* "ovis" . . . "ab oblatione"

*Trans.* "sheep" . . . "from the sacrifice"

*Note* From **Isidore of Seville,** *Etymologies* 12.1.9.


282.13
*337.31*

*Text* "canes" . . . "canor"

*Trans.* "dogs" . . . "bark"

*Note* From **Isidore of Seville,** *Etymologies* 12.2.25.


283.6–7
*338.31*

*Text* "vituli" . . . "viriditas" . . . "virgo"

*Trans.* "calves" . . . "youthfulness" . . . "maiden"

*Note* From **Isidore of Seville,** *Etymologies* 12.1.32.


284.16–17
*340.12–13*

*Text* (Secretum finis Africae manus supra idolum primum et septimum de quatuor)

*Note* See Eco 209/*245.*


*SEXT*


293.37–38
*352.25*

*Text* *Cum venerabiles*

*Trans.* *When Venerable Men*

*Note* Written by **John XXII**. The slaughter of Carpentras, not far from Avignon in southern France, occurred during the conclave which resulted in the election of John XXII to the papacy. It was a long and difficult conclave, lasting from 1314 to 1316, and beset by conflicts among the French, Italian, and Gascon cardinals. In an attempt to resolve the difficulties, Bertrand of Goth and other Gascon supporters attacked the conclave and "relieved" the cardinals of their jewels.

294.32–34
*353.26–29*

*Text* 'Corona regni de manu Dei' . . . 'Diadema imperii de manu Petri'

*Trans.* 'The crown of the realm from the hand of God' . . . 'The diadem of the empire from the hand of Peter'

*Note* This is similar to Isaiah 62:3.

295.16
*354.18–19*

*Text* taxae sacrae poenitentiariae

*Trans.* holy taxes for (obtaining) penitence

*VESPERS*

305.20
*367.9*

*Text* Favellus

*Trans.* Tawny

*COMPLINE*

308.8–18
*370.19–32*

**Text** "Cave basilischium! The rex of serpenti, et seq.

**Trans.** "Beware the basilisk! The king of serpents, so full of poison that it all shines out! What I mean, the venom, even the stink comes out and kills you! Poisons you . . . And it has black spots on its back, and a head like a cock, and half goes erect over the ground, and half on the ground like the other serpents. And it kills the weasel . . ."
"The weasel?"
"Oh! A very small animal, just a bit longer than the rat, and also called the musk-rat. And so the serpent and the toad. And when they bite it, the weasel runs to the fennel or to the sow-thistle and chews it, and comes back to the fight. And they say it generates through the eyes, but most say they are wrong."

**Note** Interestingly enough, Salvatore's sources for this fantastic description (**Isidore**, *Etymologies* 12.4.6, **Solinus**, *Collectanea* 27.51ff., and **Pliny**, *Natural History* 8.21.33) all say that the weasel kills the basilisk—and is the only thing that can!

*AFTER COMPLINE*

311.2–6
*374.12–16*

**Text** *"Historia anglorum of Bede . . . et seq.*

**Trans.** *"The History of the English People of Bede . . . And also by Bede, The Building of the Temple, The Tabernacle, The Times and Computation and Chronicle of Dionysius' Cir-*

*cle, Orthography, The System of Measures, The Life of Saint Cuthbert, The Art of Meters . . ."*

311.8
*374.18–19*

**Text** *De rhetorica cognatione, Locorum rhetoricorum distinctio*

**Trans.** *On Rhetorical Affinity, The Division of Rhetorical Arguments*

311.13
*374.23*

**Text** "Hisperica . . . famina.

**Trans.** "Irish . . . Sayings.

**Note** See "Annotated Guide."

311.16–21
*374.26–31*

**Text** *Hoc spumans mundanas obvallat Pelagus oras*
*terrestres amniosis fluctibus cudit margines.*
*Saxeas undosis molibus irruit avionias.*
*Infima bomboso vertice miscet glareas asprifero spergit spumas sulco,*
*sonoreis frequenter quatitur flabris . . .*

**Trans.** *This foaming sea encircles the world's shores,*
*Pounds with streaming waves the borders of the land.*
*It rushes into the rocky coves with walls of water,*
*Churns the depths with its resounding crest,*
*Scatters to the furrow of the stars gravel-*

> *filled waters,*
> *Frequently shaken with thundering*
> *blasts . . .*

*Note* Michael W. Herren, in the *Hisperica Famina*, pp. 92–95, gives the text of this poem with several variations. We have followed Eco's text, substituting only *astrifero* for the seemingly meaningless *asprifero*.)

311.26–29
*374.36–375.1*

*Text* 'Primitus pantorum procerum poematorum pio potissimum paternoque presertim privilegio panegiricum poemataque passim prosatori sub polo promulgatas.'

*Trans.* 'First, of all the prolonged poems, [let us sing] to our Procreator, by powerfully pious and preeminently paternal privilege, a panegyric and poems promulgated promiscuously under the polestar.'

*Note* This is taken from a letter (c. 690 A.D.) by **Aldhelm of Malmesbury** (see "Annotated Guide"), who is trying to convince a certain Ehfrith to study in England rather than in Ireland. This burst of ridiculous prose was apparently meant as proof of the superior education one would receive at Canterbury! (There are variant readings for this letter. We have supplied *hymnizemus* ("let us sing"), which Eco does not include, and we read *promulgata* for Eco's *promulgatas*.)

311.33–34
*375.6–7*

*Text Georgics . . . Epitomae*

> *Trans.* *Poems on Husbandry* . . . *Epitomes*
> (*Summaries*)

311.37–38
375.*11–12*

*Text* poema, rethoria, grama, leporia, dialecta, geometria

*Note* These terms are from the end of the section of Virgil's *Epitomae* called *De Metris*. (See "Annotated Guide" under **Virgil of Toulouse.**) Virgil lists these as the six principal studies of the many arts of learning. He then explains what he means by them: "Between *poema* and *rethoria* there is this difference, that *poema* is narrow in the variety of its content and obscure, while *rethoria*, rejoicing in its pleasantness, displays its breadth and beauty with a magnificent number of meters, feet, accents, tones and syllables. . . . *Leporia* is a rich art showing both beauty and bite on its surface." It does not, however, cling too closely to the truth. *Grama* includes the elements of reading, and *dialecta* is a study of all words, drawing them from previous authors and examining their use in sentences.

Thus the three terms *poema*, *rethoria*, and *leporia* represent literary genres (the short poem, the long poem, the elegant satire), *grama* and *dialecta*, the elementary instruction in the arts (reading, grammar, writing), and *geometria*, presumably, geometry.

312.2–3
375.*17–18*

*Text* mon, man, tonte, piron, dameth, perfellea, belgalic, margaleth, lutamiron, taminon, and raphalut."

*Note* This is also quoted verbatim from **Virgil**'s *Epitomae* 4: *De Metris*, and translation is virtually impossible. Is this part of the secret language he devised to communicate with his closest friends? (See "Annotated Guide.")

312.6–12
*375.22–28*

*Text* ignis, coquihabin, et seq.

*Trans.* ignis [fire], *coquihabin* (because it has the power of cooking raw things), *ardo* [ardor, heat], *calax* from heat, *fragon* from the crackle of the flame, *rusin* from redness, *fumaton* [smoky], *ustrax* from burning, *vitius* because it revives by itself nearly dead parts, *siluleus* because it leaps forth from flint, from which (verb) even flint is not properly derived except in so far as a spark leaps from it, and *aeneon* from the god Aeneas who dwells in it or through whom the blast is carried to the elements.

*Note* From **Virgil of Toulouse**, *Epitomae* 1: *De Sapientia*. The story of Aeneas' deification is told by the Roman poet Ovid in his *Metamorphoses* (XIV, 581 ff.).

312.17
*375.35*

*Text* ego

*Trans.* I

*Note* The vocative of "ego" is "ego."

312.21–23
*376.2–4*

*Text* cantamen, collamen, gongelamen, stemiamen, plasmamem, sonerus, alboreus, gaudifluus, glaucicomus

*Trans.* song, collection, a gathering together, formation, creation, sonorous, white, joyful, blue-grey-haired

312.29
*376.11–12*

*Text* in nomine patris et filiae

*Trans.* in the name of the Father and of the Daughter

313.20–21
*377.10–11*

*Text* HIBERNI! . . . HIBERNIA

*Trans.* IRELAND!

313.23
*377.14*

*Text* Ultima Thule

*Trans.* the Far North

*Note* See "Annotated Guide."

313.29–35
*377.21–27*

*Text* FONS . . . FONS ADAEU . . . FONS ADAE

*Trans.* BIRTHPLACE OF ADAM

314.15
*378.14*

**Text** mulier amicta sole

**Trans.** a woman robed in the sun (Revelation 12:1)

314.18,21,34
*378.16,20,36*

**Text** YSPANIA (HISPANIA)

**Trans.** SPAIN

314.37–38
*379.3–5*

**Text** LEONES. Leones: south . . . hic sunt leones.

**Trans.** LIONS. Lions: south . . . here are the lions.

315.3
*379.8*

**Text** *Canon*

**Trans.** *Canon* (*Rule*)

315.17
*379.23*

**Text** *De aspectibus*

**Trans.** *On Optics* (literally, "images")

**Note** See Eco 172.27/*199.22* and "Annotated Guide" under **Alhazen**.

316.1
*380.12*

**Text** fons paradisi

**Trans.** fountain of paradise

318.13
383.1

*Text* "Super thronos viginti quatuor."

*Trans.* "On their thrones sat the twenty-four elders." (Revelation 4:4)


320.4,11–12
385.9,19–20

*Text* IUDAEA and AEGYPTUS

*Trans.* JUDAEA and EGYPT


320.7–13,33–34
385.14–21,386.7–9

*Text* terraqueous orb . . . ANGLIA and GERMANI . . . GALLIA . . . HIBERNIA, et seq.

*Trans.* orb of earth and water . . . ENGLAND and GERMANY . . . FRANCE . . . IRELAND . . . ROME . . . SPAIN . . . AFRICA and EGYPT . . . JUDAEA and the BIRTHPLACE OF ADAM . . . GREECE

*Note* Eco has created a marvellously rich library. It owes its inspiration to medieval maps and labyrinths (and also to Argentine writer Jorge Luis Borges). It is Eco's combination of these basic medieval views of the world that is so ingenious.

The library reproduces, first of all, the world map most popular in the Christian Middle Ages, the so-called "T-O" map, which represented the world as a flat disk of land completely encircled by the ocean. At the top, where North appears on maps today, the medieval cartographer placed East (hence our word "orientation"), so that Paradise would have the position of greatest importance (the *Fons Adae* of the library, through which one entered). The O of the T-O map is formed by the circle of the ocean, the T by the intersection of the main waterways, the Mediterranean Sea and the Nile and Don rivers. The T also divides the land into the three continents: Asia on the top (East), Africa on the lower right (South-West) and Europe on the lower left (North-West).

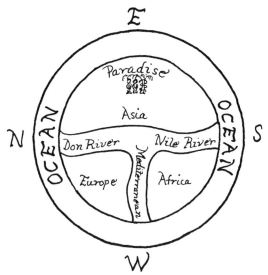

"In short," says Adso, "when we later perfected the map definitively we were convinced that the library was truly laid out and arranged according to the image of the terraqueous orb."

Eco's library is also derived from medieval labyrinths. There was, in fact, a maze 35 feet in diameter on the floor of Rheims Cathedral in France, dated 1211, which had the precise form of the library. It was arbitrarily destroyed in 1779, when a conceited canon objected to the noise made by those who traced its course during his services.

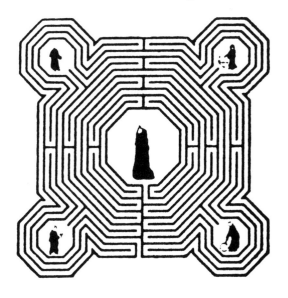

This labyrinth, combined with the notion of the T-O map, was placed by Eco in a structure resembling the thirteenth century Castel del Monte in Apulia. This fortress was erected by Frederick II on a bluff near the Adriatic. It is an octagonal structure, like Eco's Aedificium, but has octagonal towers at all eight angles. It was not a library, but a royal residence, with an inner octagonal courtyard. Built of white stone, it is especially ghostly when seen by moonlight.

320.23–27
*385.34–386.3*

*Text* "quarta Acaiae"

*Trans.* "the fourth room of Greece"

*Note* "Achaeans" appears as one of three names for the Greeks in Homer's *Iliad* and *Odyssey;* in classical times, "Achaea" ("Acaia") indicated a particular district of southern Greece. The name "Greeks," incidentally, is also a synecdoche—a figure of speech in which a part is used for the whole: the Italians, familiar with the Graeci, a tribe of Greeks living in Italy, subsequently referred to all Greeks by that name.

322.5–6
*386.20–21*

*Text* terra incognita

*Trans.* an unknown land

*Note* See Eco 184.10/*214.23*.

322.21
*388.2*

***Text** Speculum amoris*

***Trans.*** *The Mirror of Love*


322.31–32
*388.15*

***Text*** "De te fabula narratur"

***Trans.*** "The story is about you"

***Note*** See Eco 241.12/*286.16.*


323.30
*389.25–26*

***Text*** "nigra et amara"

***Trans.*** "black and bitter"


323.34
*389.30*

***Text*** *Liber continens*

***Trans.*** *Comprehensive Book*

***Note*** See "Annotated Guide" under **Abu-Bakr Muhammed.**


325.17
*391.30*

***Text*** "complexio venerea"

***Trans.*** "condition (dilemma) of sexuality"

*NIGHT*


328.20
*396.5*

***Text*** 'catus'

***Trans.*** 'cat'

328.23
396.8

*Text* *De legibus*

*Trans.* *On Laws*

329.22
397.17

*Text* *Super illius specula*

*Trans.* **Upon the Images** (literally, "mirrors") *of Him* (we reflect in grief)

*Note* Written by **John XXII** in 1326. By the "mirrors of Him" John means men, whom God created in His own image "to be first on earth, adorned with divine virtues." John goes on at length to describe man as God intended him—and grieves over how far he has fallen.

"Unhappily," John says, "we now know that there are many who, Christian in name only, have abandoned the first light of truth and enter into a pact with death; for they make sacrifice to devils, adore them, and create images of them." He goes on to discuss, and condemn, various forms of devil worship.

Fifth Day

*PRIME*

338.36
407.31

*Text* "Quorundam exigit"

*Trans.* "(The blindness) of certain men demands"

*Note* This bull by **John XXII** (October 7, 1317) discusses the habit worn by the Franciscans and variations that have entered into it, and then settles into a discussion of Franciscan poverty. John allows the Franciscans storehouses of supplies, a violation of the strictest interpretation of poverty, and ends by saying that "poverty is indeed great, but chastity is greater; the greatest good of all is obedience if it is kept inviolate. . . . For the first is concerned with things, the second with the flesh, but the third with the mind and the soul."

339.10
*408.10*

*Text Ad conditorem canonum*

*Trans. To the Founder of the Rules*

*Note* Written by **John XXII**, December 8, 1322. See *Note* 55.38/*59.7–8*. John again discusses Franciscan poverty and makes a distinction between *usus*, simple use, and *dominium*, possession.

The Franciscan chapter at Perugia had met in May of 1322 and had declared Franciscan poverty as *simplex usus facti:* as a horse has "use" of the oats he eats without possessing them, just so the friar has use of his food, drink, clothing, etc. without possession, that is, he has *simplex usus facti* (simple use in fact) without *ius utendi* (the right of use).

In this bull, John gave to the Friars, against their will, possession of the things they used, which had formerly been considered the possessions of the Pope. This was in outright opposition to Nicholas III's bull of 1279 (*Exiit qui seminat*). See Eco p. 341/ *411*.

339.18
*408.20*

*Text Cum inter nonnullos*

*Trans. Since among some (learned men)*

*Note* See *Note* 13.18/6.2–3. *Cum inter nonnullos* was a very strong and dogmatic statement on the part of **John XXII** on the poverty of Christ, declaring it heretical to claim, as did the Franciscans, that Christ and his apostles did not have possession of those things they used. (With *Ad conditorem canonum* he had declared the Franciscans owners; now he was declaring them heretics!)

339.27
*408.31*

*Text* inimicus pacis

*Trans.* an enemy of peace

339.33
*408.38*

*Text Quia quorundam (mentes)*

*Trans. Because the minds of certain men*

*Note* Written by **John XXII**, November 10, 1324. John here asserts that his *Ad conditorem canonum* and *Cum inter nonnullos* in no way contradicted the teachings of his predecessors on the subject of Christ's poverty, and affirms the Pope's right to decide matters of doctrine.

Its main thrust is again the subject of Christ's poverty, and again he denies it. He goes even further in declaring that possession is better than the lack of it, and that less is not better than more. He affirms, in fact, the sanctity of property.

341.7
*410.25–26*

**Text** "in bonis nostris"

**Trans.** "among our goods"

341.21–23
*411.5–8*

**Text** ius poli . . . ius fori

**Trans.** the law of heaven (Church law) . . . the law of the marketplace (secular law)

341.35
*411.23*

See also
*342/412*

**Text** *Exiit qui seminat*

**Trans.** *He Has Gone Out Who Sows*

**Note** This bull was actually issued by Nicholas III (not Nicholas II, as Eco says) on August 14, 1279. In it Nicholas eulogizes the Franciscan order, the seed that was sown by the sower in such good soil that it brings forth abundant fruit. Unfortunately, he says, inferior plants have crept in which must be weeded out.

The most important section of the bull deals with the question of poverty. Gregory IX (*Quo elongati*, 1229) had used the term *usus rerum* to signify use of things without possession. Nicholas clarifies the distinction by saying that the Friars had not *usus iuris*, use of right or possession, but rather *usus facti*, use in fact. Everything was held, possessed by the Roman Church, i.e. the Pope. The Friars had only the use.

Nicholas ends the bull by saying that its contents are inviolable and eternal and cannot be disputed on pain of excommunication—a warning that does little to intimidate John!

## TERCE

353.3–4
*425.5–6*

**Text** nomina sunt consequentia rerum

**Trans.** names are the consequences of things

353.14–15
*425.18–21*

**Text** "nomen" . . . "nomos" . . . nomina . . . ad placitum

**Trans.** "name" . . . "law" . . . names . . . by agreement

## SEXT

362.17
*436.20*

**Text** *De plantis libri tres*

*Trans.* *Three Books on Plants*

362.19
*436.22*

*Text* *Thesaurus herbarum*

*Trans.* *A Treasury of Herbs*

*NONES*

370.29
*447.9–10*

*Text* *Sancta Romana*

*Trans.* *The Holy Roman* (*Church*)

*Note* Written by **John XXII**, December 30, 1317. John talks about various splinter groups of Franciscans, whom he calls Fraticelli (little brothers), fratres de paupere vita (brothers of the poor life), bizochi, beguines, etc. He declares these new congregations heretical and orders them suppressed and eliminated.

372.17
*449.14*

*Text* de dicto

*Trans.* of speech

375.2–3
*452.20–21*

*Text* And you were to me dilectissimo. . . . Qui non habet caballum vadat cum pede.

*Trans.* And you were to me very beloved. But you know the chief constable's family. A man who has no horse goes on foot.

*Note* The last sentence is a reminder of **John XXII**'s cunning betrayal of Cardinal Orsini. See Eco 292/*351*.

375.7–11
*452.26–31*

*Text* "What do I know, lord, what all these heresias are called . . . Patarini, gazzesi, et seq.

*Trans.* "What do I know, lord, what all these heresies are called . . . Patarines, Gazzesi, Lyonists, Arnoldists, Speronists, Circumcised . . . I am not an educated man. I sinned with no malice, and Signor Bernard the Most Magnificent knows it, and I am hoping in his pardon in the name of the Father, and of the Son, and of the Holy Ghost . . ."

379.6
*457.21*

*Text* Domini canes

*Trans.* the Lord's dogs

383.34
*463.22–23*

*Text* 'Salve Regina'

*Trans.* 'Hail, (Holy) Queen'

*Note* This hymn, written around 1100, perhaps by Hermannus Contractus, was a great favorite in the Middle Ages.

384.25
*464.21*

*Text* planta Dei pullulans in radice fidei

*Trans.* plant of God sprouting in the soil of faith

*Note* This is reminiscent of Isaiah 11:1–2: "And there shall come forth a rod out of the stem of Jesse, and a branch shall grow out of his roots: And the spirit of the Lord shall rest upon him, the spirit of wisdom and understanding, the spirit of counsel and might, the spirit of knowledge and of the fear of the Lord."

388.19–23
469.9–14

*Text* Abigor, pecca pro nobis, et seq.

*Trans.* Abigor, sin for us . . . Amon, have mercy on us . . . Samael, free us from good . . . Belial, have mercy . . . Focalor, attend to my corruption . . . Haborym, we damn the lord . . . Zaebos, open my ass . . . Leonard, sprinkle me with your seed and I shall be stained . . .

*Note* This is a hideous parody of a litany: "pecca pro nobis" for "ora pro nobis" (pray for us), "libera nos a bono" for "libera nos a malo" ("deliver us from evil" from the Lord's Prayer), "anum meum aperies" for "labia mea aperies" (open my lips), "asperge me spermate tuo et inquinabor" for "asperges me hyssopo et mundabor" (sprinkle me with marjoram and I shall be clean), etc.

389.14
470.11

*Text* cingulum diaboli

*Trans.* devil's bond (literally "belt")

*Note* See William's speech on inquisitions on 59.32/*63.34.*


## SIXTH DAY

*MATINS*

411/*497*
(subtitle)

*Text* sederunt

*Trans.* were seated

412.13–21
*498.25–32*

*Text* *Sederunt principes*
*et adversus me*
*loquebantur, iniqui*
*persecuti sunt me.*
*Adiuva me, Domine*
*Deus meus, salvum me*
*fac propter magnam misericordiam tuam.*

*Trans.* *The princes were seated*
*and were speaking*
*against me. The wicked*
*have persecuted me.*
*Help me, Lord,*
*My God; make me*
*safe because of your great*
*compassion.*

*Note* This hymn is taken from Psalm 119.

412.38
*499.14*

*Text* "Ave Maria"s

*Trans.* "Hail Mary"'s

## PRIME

422.2
*510.29*

*Text* Abbas agraphicus

*Trans.* the Abbot who could not write

424.34
*514.13*

*Text* minimas differentias odorum

*Trans.* smallest differences in smells

## TERCE

426/*516*
(subtitle)

*Text* "Dies irae"

*Trans.* "Day of Wrath"

*Note* This sequence, which depicts the horrors of the Last Judgment, is sung as part of the Mass for the Dead. Originally it was also an Advent hymn, and so the "Dies Irae" that Adso hears is doubly appropriate.

429.17
*520.13–14*

*Text* "Age primum et septimum de quatuor"

*Trans.* "Move the first and seventh of the four"

430.13
*521.18–19*

*Text* vitra ad legendum

*Trans.* glasses for reading

*Note* See Eco 86/*97* and *173*/*200*.

431.2
*522.15*

*Text* nigra sed formosa

*Trans.* black but beautiful

*Note* From Song of Songs 1:5

431.30–31
*523.13*

*Text* unico homine regente

*Trans.* with only one man in control

*Note* See Eco 17.25/*11.14*

431.33
*523.16*

*Text* amicta sole

*Trans.* robed in the sun

*Note* See the *mulier* on 175.22–23/*203*.7.

432.4
*523.28*

*Text Pentagonum Salomonis*

*Trans. The Pentagon of Solomon*

*Note* See Eco 75.5/*83*.7.

434.4
*526.11–12*

*Text* mors est quies viatoris, finis est omnis laboris

*Trans.* death is the traveller's rest, the end of all his labor

*Note* See Eco 64.28–29/70.2–3.

435.1
527.20

*Text* "Ut cachinnis dissolvatur, torqueatur rictibus!"

*Trans.* "Let him be convulsed with laughter, let him be twisted into a gaping grin!"

435.14–19
527.35–528.3

*Text* Lacrimosa dies illa
qua resurget ex favilla
iudicando homo reus:
huic ergo parce deus!
Pie Iesu domine
dona eis requiem.

*Trans.* Rich in tears will be that day
on which will rise from the ashes
the man condemned for judgment:
Spare him then, O God!
Gracious Lord Jesus,
Give them rest.

## AFTER TERCE

437.6
530.17

*Text* **Coena Cypriani**

*Trans.* Cyprian's Dinner

*Note* See "Annotated Guide."

437.11
*530.23*

*Text* ioca monachorum

*Trans.* jokes of monks

*SEXT*

439.9–14
*533.10–15*

*Text*  I. ar. de dictis cuiusdam stulti
 II. syr. libellus alchemicus aegypt.
III. Expositio Magistri Alcofribae de coena beati Cypriani Cartaginensis Episcopi
IV. Liber acephalus de stupris virginum et meretricum amoribus

*Trans.*  I. Arabic: On the Sayings of Some Fool
 II. Syriac: A Little Egyptian Book on Alchemy
III. Master Alcofriba's Explanation of the Dinner of the Blessed Cyprian, Bishop of Carthage
IV. A Book (untitled) on the Debauches of Maidens and the Love Affairs of Whores

440.33
*535.10–11*

*Text* Abbas agraphicus

*Trans.* the Abbot who could not write. See Eco 422/*510*.

441.10
*535.30*

*Text Firma cautela*

*Trans. With Firm Precaution*

*Note* There is a misprint in the text. The bull is by **Boniface VIII**, not Boniface VII. See Eco 52/*54*.

443.15,28
*538.15,30*

*Text* Charta lintea

*Trans.* Linen paper

*NONES*

444.18
*540.4–5*

*Text* —vox, flatus, pulsus—

*Trans.* —voice, breath, beat—

*Note* This presumably refers to the elements of human speech. *Vox* is the vowel; *flatus,* the aspirated consonant; and *pulsus,* the unaspirated consonant.

*AFTER COMPLINE*

457.18–26
*555.30–556.3*

*Text* 'tertius equi'

*Trans.* 'the third of the horse'

*Note* See Eco 219.18–20/*258.30–33*.

457.30–31
*556.6–7*

*Text* suppositio materialis, the discourse is presumed de dicto and not de re

*Trans.* the material supposition, the discourse is presumed about the word itself and not about the thing for which it stands

*Note* Material supposition occurs, according to **William of Occam** (*Summa totius logicae,* I, 63, 67—See "Annotated Guide"), when a term stands for the vocal or written word rather than for that which it signifies. In the proposition " 'Man' is a noun," man stands for itself (the word "man") and not for what it signifies (the concept man). Examples of material supposition are: 'Man' is singular, 'Man is an animal' is a true proposition, 'Man' is a one-syllable word, 'Man' is a three-letter word.

458.5
556.23–24

*Text* 'primum et septimum de quatuor'

*Trans.* 'the first and the seventh of the four'

*Note* See Eco 209.1–9/245.34–246.7.

458.8
556.26–27

*Text* Super thronos viginti quatuor!

*Trans.* On their thrones sat the twenty-four elders!

*Note* See Eco 170.8/196.21.

## SEVENTH DAY
Saturday

*NIGHT*

475.29
579.2

*Text* terra incognita

*Trans.* an unknown land

*Note* See Eco 184.10/*214.23* and 322.5–6/*386.20–21*.

477.10
*580.38*

*Text* libellus

*Trans.* little book

478.2
*581.37–38*

*Text* de toto corpore fecerat linguam

*Trans.* had made a tongue out of his entire body

478.5
*582.3*

*Text* 'Miserere'

*Trans.* 'Have mercy'

478.35–36
*583.3*

*Text* 'Hic sunt leones'

*Trans.* 'Here are the lions'

*Note* See Eco 314.37–38/*379.3–5*.

*NIGHT*

483.4
*587.28*

*Text* YSPANIA (HISPANIA)

*Trans.* SPAIN

*Note* See Eco 314.18/*378.16*

492.29–30
*600.1–2*

**Text** Er muoz gelîchesame die leiter abe-
werfen, sô er an ir ufgestigen.

**Trans.** One must cast away, as it were, the
ladder, so that he may begin to ascend it.

493.22–23
*601.4–5*

**Text** "Non in commotione, non in commotione Dominus."

**Trans.** "The Lord is not in confusion, not
in confusion."

**Note** From 1 Kings 19:11–12. Elijah, after
slaughtering the prophets of Baal, fled to
Horeb, the mountain of God, for refuge. As
he stood on the mount, "the Lord passed
by, and a great and strong wind rent the
mountains, and brake in pieces the rocks
before the Lord; but the Lord was not in
the wind: and after the wind an earthquake;
but the Lord was not in the earthquake
(*commotione*): And after the earthquake a
fire; but the Lord was not in the fire: and
after the fire a still small voice."

*LAST PAGE*

498.5
*606.16*

**Text** res nullius

**Trans.** no one's property

500.17
*609.13*

**Text** disiecta membra

**Trans.** scattered fragments

**Note** See Eco 47.17/*48.17*.

500.23
*609.21*

**Text** incipit

**Trans.** beginning

**Note** "Incipit" literally means "here begins" and formed the introductory part of
medieval manuscripts.

500.33–34
*609.33*

**Text** Tolle et lege.

**Trans.** Take and read.

**Note** Saint Augustine (354–430 A.D.) tells
of the precise moment of his conversion to
Christianity in his *Confessions* (VIII, 12).
While weeping over his unworthiness, he
heard a child's voice chanting, "Tolle, lege;
tolle, lege." He interpreted this as a direct
command from God to take the Book and
read the first chapter he found. When he
opened the Bible, the first words he saw
were "not in rioting and drunkenness, not
in chambering and wantonness, not in strife
and envying. But put ye on the Lord Jesus
Christ, and make not provision for the flesh,
to fulfil the lusts thereof (Romans 13:13–
14)." He read no further. Instantly, he says,

serenity filled his heart, and the darkness of doubt disappeared.

501.20
*610.24*

*Text* Est ubi gloria nunc Babyloniae?

*Trans.* Where is the glory of Babylon now?

*Note* From **Bernard of Cluny,** *De contemptu mundi*, I, 933 (See "Annotated Guide.") This is reminiscent of Revelation 14:8.

501.24–25
*610.29–31*

*Text* O quam salubre, quam iucundum et suave est sedere in solitudine et tacere et loqui cum Deo!

*Trans.* O how healthy, how pleasant, and how sweet it is to sit in solitude, to be silent and to talk with God!

*Note* This is taken from the *Soliloquium Animae* of **Thomas à Kempis** (See "Annotated Guide"), who is also quoted by Eco in his introduction, p.5/xix. **Thomas à Kempis'** dates are c.1380–1471. Speaking of Adso's manuscript, Eco himself says, "the date of the author's writing . . . is uncertain. Inasmuch as he describes himself as a novice in 1327 and says he is close to death as he writes his memoirs, we can calculate roughly that the manuscript was written in the last or next-to-last decade of the fourteenth century (p.4/xvi)." Unless **Thomas à Kempis** wrote his *Soliloquium* in near infancy, it would be impossible for Adso to have read it! Eco makes very few such mistakes.

501.29
*610.35–36*

**Text** Gott ist ein lauter Nichts, ihn rührt kein Nun noch Hier.

**Trans.** God is pure nothingness, touched by neither Now nor Here.

**Note** This text occurs, as is, in Angelus Silesius (1624–1677). He is, of course, too late for Adso to quote, but the notions contained in this quotation all occur in the sermons of the German mystic Meister **Eckhart** (c.1260–1328). See "Annotated Guide." Eckhart speaks of "ein lauter Nichts" (sermon 4, Blakney, *Meister Eckhart: A Modern Translation*) as a state of pure nothingness, i.e. a state of perfect quiet and recollection where nothing will distract the soul from contemplation of God. Elsewhere (sermon 15), he says that the intellect can only know God when detached from the Here and Now (Hier und Nun). And so Adso, in his old age, looks for this God, a God of complete absorption and total tranquillity. See Adso's own remarks on 11.10–13/*3.12–15*.

502.2–3
*611.15–16*

**Text** stat rosa pristina nomine, nomina nuda tenemus.

**Trans.** Yesterday's rose endures in its name, we hold empty names.

*Note* From **Bernard of Cluny,** *De contemptu mundi* I.952. This line is from the first book of Bernard of Cluny's *De contemptu mundi.* The poem, a long and bitter satire on the failings and corruption of contemporary ecclesiastical institutions, emphasizes the transitory nature of human existence, the basic futility of human endeavor. Only Bernard's firm faith in a better afterlife rescues his poem from a tone of unremitting despair. After man, says Bernard, there is only ash, dissolved, as it were, in the breath of the whirlwind. What was once a blossom is now dung. Where now is the glory of Babylon, where Nebuchadnezzar, Darius, Cyrus? Only their former fame is left; the men themselves rot. Where now are the heroic deeds of men, where Cicero's noble oratory, where the patriotism of Cato? *Stat rosa pristina nomine, nomina nuda tenemus:* yesterday's rose endures in its name; we hold empty names.

The library, built up over centuries, lies in ruins. Even Adso's efforts to reconstruct it amount to nothing more than a collection of scattered fragments. The library, for which men were willing to kill, is now nothing but ashes and titles.

# For Those Who Have Finished
# *THE NAME OF THE ROSE*

*Some books are to be tasted, others to be swallowed, and some few to be chewed and digested: that is, some books are to be read only in parts, others to be read, but not curiously, and some few to be read wholly, and with diligence and attention.*

Francis Bacon: *Of Studies*

*The Name of the Rose* by any other name might have been called the "Apocalypse of Adso." For, as Alinardo declares to William in his inspired delirium, behind the crimes of the nameless abbey and the labyrinthine events of November 1327 lies a world whose key is the Book of Revelation, possibly the most exquisite of all Christian, Jewish, Greek and Roman works of "vision" literature. Known also as the Apocalypse of John, the last book of the Bible describes a vision, both cosmic and historic, of God's imminent destruction of the sinful world, the resurrection of the faithful, and the coming of a new heaven and earth in which God will dwell with mankind forever. This book, with its alternating tone of terror and hope, its repetitious sequences of apocalyptic vision within apocalyptic vision, and its familiar yet tantalizingly obscure symbols, permeates *The Name of the Rose* as seductively as the aroma of hallucinogenic herbs pervades the library after dark.

"It was a beautiful morning at the end of November." The year is 1327. The novel opens on a Sunday, presumably the first day of Advent, the beginning of the liturgical year and a period of anticipation when the Church awaits the coming, or advent, of Christ. Advent became, during the papacy of Gregory I (590–604), a four-week cycle to represent the fourfold coming of Christ—his coming in the flesh on Christmas, at the hour of a man's death, at the fall of Jerusalem, and finally on the Last Day, the Day of Judgment.

On this particular Sunday in 1327, the whole monastery seems unduly preoccupied with Christ's final coming and the arrival of the much-dreaded millennium. The Antichrist, says Alinardo, "is about to come, the millennium is past; we await him. . . ." "But the millennium was three hundred years ago," says William, "and he did not come then. . . ." "The millennium is not calculated from the death of Christ," answers Alinardo, "but from the donation of Constantine, three centuries later. Now it is a thousand years. . . ." Thus the scene is carefully being set for the apocalyptic events that are to take place in the abbey.

Scenes from the Book of Revelation, majestic and horrifying, are carved in stone around the entrance to the abbey's Church. Apocalyptic verses appear on the scrolls above the doorways of the library's many rooms. In the library itself, Adso receives strange visions inspired by illuminated manuscripts of the Apocalypse—of the "woman robed in the sun," the red dragon "dragging after him the stars of the sky," and the whore of Babylon. William and Adso discover, too, that the abbey's library houses the largest collection of copies of the Apocalypse in Christendom "and an immense quantity of commentaries on the subject."

Adso of Melk, Eco's narrator, is himself an apocalyptic figure, a combination of at least two important figures in the history of "vision" literature. His name, as Jorge points out, recalls that of Adso of Montier-en-Der, the tenth century author of the *Libellus de Antichristo* (*Short Book on the Antichrist*), one of the most influential medieval commentaries on the Apocalypse. Adso is likewise an avatar of John, the author of Revelation. Gazing for the first time at the entrance to the Church, Adso finds himself transported by the Apocalyptic drama above him—"The Seated One" triumphant in judgment over those defeated at Armageddon. Like John, Adso refers to his experience as a vision: "I seemed to hear (or did I really hear?) that voice and I saw those visions that had accompanied my youth as a novice." He goes on to paraphrase the Book of Revelation:

> I heard a voice mighty as a trumpet that said, "Write in a book what you now see" (and this is what I am doing), and I saw seven golden candlesticks and in the midst of the candlesticks One like unto the son of man, his breast girt with a golden girdle, his head and hair white as purest wool, his eyes as a flame of fire, his feet like unto fine brass, as if they burned in a furnace. . . .

It is at this point that Adso realizes that "the vision was speaking precisely of what was happening in the abbey," and that he and William have come there "in order to witness a great and celestial massacre."

Adso experiences other visions in *The Name of the Rose:* his hallucination in the library and his dream during the chanting of the ominous "Dies Irae" ("Day of Wrath"), both smaller apocalyptic visions within the larger. John, the author of the Book of Revelation, and Adso are, moreover, passive observers within their own works—witnesses who receive their revelation (as they themselves attest) not from God directly, but through an intermediary. The counterpart to John's "One like unto the son of man" is undoubtedly William of Baskerville, Adso's guide through the intersecting spiritual and physical labyrinths.

Throughout the novel, self-styled prophets and militant millennarians repeat the threats and predictions found in the

Book of Revelation. Salvatore's expression "Penitenziagite!" ("Repent!") recalls the admonition of John the Baptist, "Repent ye: for the kingdom of heaven is at hand" (Matthew 3:2) as well as the calls to penitence in chapters 2 and 3 of Revelation: "Remember therefore from whence thou art fallen, and repent" (2:5), "Repent; or else I will come unto thee quickly" (2:16), and "Remember therefore how thou hast received and heard, and hold fast, and repent" (3:3). Ubertino awaits the Antichrist: "We have reached the sixth era of human history, when two Antichrists will appear, the mystic Antichrist and the Antichrist proper. And this is happening now." There follows a discussion on the identity of the two Antichrists. Alinardo views all the murders in the abbey as manifestations of the coming of the millennium. And, on the basis of his raving, William seeks clues to the solution of the murders in the seven trumpets of the Apocalypse. And finally there is Jorge's sermon in which he declares that the Antichrist is the symbol of man's pride which compels him "to break the seals of the books that are not his to see."

Eco's conscious structuring of *The Name of the Rose* according to apocalyptic patterns is further revealed in his use of numbers. In the Book of Revelation, John declares that he was caught up by his vision on the Lord's Day (1:10) and then proceeds to organize his narrative into a seven-fold series of sevens—seven seals, seven trumpets, seven signs, seven bowls of wrath, etc.— with each septet developing out of the other in a continuous and unified pattern. Similarly, Adso experiences his first vision on Sunday, the Lord's Day, and describes the unfolding events over a seven-day period. To apocalyptic writers, the seven-day cycle represented the dissolution of the material universe, the end of history. Pierre Olieu, the Spiritual Franciscan who influenced Ubertino, divided history into seven periods and declared that St. Francis, the angel of the sixth seal, had ushered in the Sixth Age in which "spiritual men"—distinguished by their poverty—would do battle against the lascivious Church, which Olieu's followers were later to call the Whore of Avignon! Jorge, too, in his sermon, warns that six days of natural disasters in the universe will culminate in the destruction of the world followed by the day of judgment on the seventh. In *The Name of the Rose*, the burning of the library occurs, appropriately enough, during the dark hours of the morning of the seventh day when the very elements appear to conspire in the spread of the flames and the devastation of the abbey.

Eco is fascinated by what he calls the "play of empty oppositions" in the structure of Revelation, a text in which there is "no exact solution": "Revelation becomes an instrument with which to contest every already established meaning" (Eco, *FMR*, 2, p. 88). *The Name of the Rose*, like a self-conscious Apocalypse, presents apparent oppositions (heresy and orthodoxy, whore and virgin, Devil and God) that on closer inspection are seen to be mirror images of one another.

Like the Apocalypse and other works of "vision" literature, the short fiction of Jorge Luis Borges has also influenced *The Name of the Rose*. Borges, a former Director of the National Library in Buenos Aires, appears in the figure of Jorge of Burgos, who is revealed, in the end, to be the real power in the abbey's library. Several of Borges' most striking images mingle with those of Revelation in Eco's novel. For example, both Eco and Borges consider the mirror to be a door, a passage between two worlds or two images of reality, like the door opened in heaven through which John was able to see "The Seated One" on his throne (Revelation 4). In *The Name of the Rose*, the mirrored door leads into the *Secretum*, which means both "secret" and "a secluded room for reading the Bible." Yet the books in this room are not Bibles, but the forbidden works of the infidels. Thus the mirrored door represents the passage between the Christian world and the pagan world, between past and future, darkness and enlightenment, life and death—a door through which only three pass successfully in *The Name of the Rose:* Adso, Jorge, and William.

Behind the mirror a man inevitably finds his double, his other self. When Adso first comes upon the mirror in the library, he recoils at the sight of his own image, enlarged and distorted, and thinks it a devil. When he and William later pass through the mirror and enter the *Secretum*, William finds his own reflection, Jorge, sitting there awaiting his arrival. Adso describes their meeting:

> I realized, with a shudder, that at this moment these two men, arrayed in a mortal conflict, were admiring each other, as if each had acted only to win the other's applause. The thought crossed my mind that the artifices Berengar used to seduce Adelmo, and the simple and natural acts with which the girl had aroused my passion and my desire, were nothing compared with the cleverness and mad skill each used to conquer the other, nothing compared with the act of seduction going on before my eyes at that moment, which had unfolded over seven days, each of the two interlocutors making, as it were, mysterious appointments with the other, each secretly aspiring to the other's approbation, each fearing and hating the other.

The two face each other in their final confrontation, each bursting with pride at his own cleverness. Jorge tries to dazzle William with his subtle tricks—the mirror, the herbs, the poison. William, on the other hand, wants Jorge to know every step of the process which has led him to the *Secretum*, yearns to lead him through the twisted labyrinth of erroneous reasoning which has brought him finally to a dead end. "Because of a remark of Alinardo's," says William, "I was convinced the series of crimes followed the sequence of the seven trumpets of the Apocalypse. . . . I conceived a false pattern to interpret the moves of the guilty man, and the guilty man fell in with it." And yet the final clue comes quite by accident in a chance remark of Adso's, giving William the key to entering the finis Africae. "I cannot follow you," Jorge says. "You are proud to show me how, following the dictates of your reason, you arrived at me, and yet you have shown me you arrived here by following a false reasoning. What do you mean to say to me?"

Indeed, we might ask Umberto Eco the same question.

He has filled the pages of his "immense acrostic" with false starts and blind alleys. The Apocalypse, seemingly so vital to the unravelling of the crimes, is revealed in the end to have little or no bearing on their solution. Nor do the endless debates on Franciscan spirituality and poverty. Instead, what we find at the center of the labyrinth is a demented old man hiding the last copy in Europe of Aristotle's treatise on comedy. An evil prophet obsessed with apocalyptic lakes of fire and convinced that laughter is "weakness, corruption, the foolishness of our flesh," Jorge has concealed at all costs the book he believes will undermine the gravity of truth and destroy the world. And, when he realizes that he can conceal it no longer, the crazed monk devours the fatal scroll just as John was commanded to do in Apocalypse 10. Like the devil he fears, Jorge "lives in darkness." He never laughs until the moment of his death, when he swallows the pages of Aristotle and "returns whence he came." Jorge dies in YSPANIA, the land of his birth and the destination of that fateful journey from which he returned with the book of Aristotle and innumerable texts and commentaries on the Apocalypse. (No less ironically, William, the scholar who seems immune to others' obsession with the prophecies of the Book of Revelation, uses Jorge's own apocalyptic vocabulary when he calls the old man the Devil and the Antichrist; and he, the scientist who seems to have mastered the most abstruse medical theories of Aristotle and Platearius, will himself fall prey to the Black Death that ravaged Europe from 1347 to 1350.)

Finally, after demonstrating the irrelevance of the apocalyptic clues, showing that most of the murders were not murders at all, and revealing the demonic Jorge as William's darker self, Eco plays on his readers one last trick. The semiotic sorcerer, who has conjured up an elaborate labyrinth with hidden passages, a secret room, and a distorting mirror, stages the ultimate disappearing act: the abbey, with its library and its marvelous collection of books, is engulfed by flames and becomes a "horrid replica of Armageddon."

And what message are we to derive from Eco's mock

apocalypse? Are we to believe Eco when he says that *The Name of the Rose* is simply "a tale of books, not of everyday worries . . . gloriously lacking in any relevance for our day, atemporally alien to our hopes and our certainties?" Are we to accept the burning of the library as sad but inevitable—the passing away of one world before the emergence of another? Are we to interpret the echo of Jorge's laughter as the voice of Eco himself? Adso's rose, as Eco's own nostalgia? Eco does not say: in every interview and public appearance, he remains silent when asked to interpret *The Name of the Rose.* Instead, with both erudition and wit, Eco gives us a glimpse into "the disaster of an aging world," fully aware as an historian that the close scrutiny of the particulars of any era leads often, if only accidentally, to a universal truth.

# Works by Umberto Eco

## In English Translation

*The Picture History of Inventions: From Plough to Polaris.* Edited with G. Zorzoli. Translated by Anthony Lawrence. New York: Macmillan, 1963.

*The People's Comic Book: Red Women's Detachment, Hot on the Trail, and Other Chinese Comics.* Edited with Jean Chesneaux and Gino Nebiolo. Translated by Frances Frenaye. New York: Anchor Press, 1973.

*The Role of the Reader: Explorations in the Semiotics of Texts.* Bloomington: Indiana University Press, 1979.

*The Name of the Rose.* Translated by William Weaver. New York: Harcourt Brace Jovanovich, 1983.

*Postscript to "The Name of the Rose."* Translated by William Weaver. New York: Harcourt Brace Jovanovich, 1984.

*Art and Beauty in the Middle Ages.* Translated by Hugh Bredin. New Haven: Yale University Press, 1986.

*Travels in Hyperreality.* Edited by Helen Wolff and Kurt Wolff. Translated by William Weaver. New York: Harcourt Brace Jovanovich, 1986.

*The Aesthetics of Thomas Aquinas.* Translated by Hugh Bredin. Cambridge: Harvard University Press, 1988.

*Foucault's Pendulum.* Translated by William Weaver. New York: Harcourt Brace Jovanovich, 1989.

*The Aesthetics of Chaosmos: The Middle Ages of James Joyce.* Translated by Ellen Esrock. Cambridge: Harvard University Press, 1989.

*The Bomb and the General.* Translated by William Weaver. Illustrated by Eugenio Carmi. New York: Harcourt Brace Jovanovich, 1989.

*The Open Work.* Translated by Anna Cancogni. Introduced by David Robey. Cambridge: Harvard University Press, 1989.

*Misreadings.* Translated by William Weaver. New York: Harcourt Brace and Co., 1993.

*The Search for the Perfect Language.* Translated by James Fentress. Oxford: Blackwell, 1994.
*How to Travel with a Salmon and Other Essays.* Translated by William Weaver. New York: Harcourt Brace and Co., 1994.
*The Island of the Day Before.* Translated by William Weaver. New York: Harcourt Brace and Co., 1995.
*Serendipities: Language and Lunacy.* Translated by William Weaver. New York: Columbia University Press, 1998.

## In English

*A Theory of Semiotics.* Bloomington: Indiana University Press, 1976.
*Semiotics and the Philosophy of Language.* Bloomington: Indiana University Press, 1984.
*Sign of the Three: Dupin, Holmes, Peirce.* Edited with Thomas A. Sebeok. Bloomington: Indiana University Press, 1984.
"Waiting for the Millennium." *FMR (Franco Maria Ricci)* 2 (July 1984): 63–92.
*Meaning and Mental Representations.* Edited with Marco Santambrogio and Patrizia Vio. Bloomington: Indiana University Press, 1988.
*The Three Astronauts.* New York: Harcourt Brace Jovanovich, 1989.
*On the Medieval Theory of Signs.* Edited with Costantino Marmo. Philadelphia: John Benjamins, 1989.
*The Limits of Interpretation.* Bloomington: Indiana University Press, 1990.
*Interpretation and Overinterpretation.* With Richard Rorty, Jonathan Culler, and Christine Brooke-Rose. Edited by Stefan Collini. Cambridge: Cambridge University Press, 1992.
*Apocalypse Postponed: Essays.* Bloomington: Indiana University Press, 1994.
*Six Walks in the Fictional Woods.* Cambridge: Harvard University Press, 1994.

## In Italian

*Il problema estetico in San Tommaso.* Edizioni di Filosofia, 1956. Second edition published as *Il problema estetico in Tommaso d'Aquino.* Milan: Bompiani, 1970.
*Filosofi in libertà.* Turin: Taylor, 1958. Second edition, 1959.

*Momenti e problema di storia dell'estetica.* Contributor with others. Milan: Marzorati, 1959.

*Storia figurata delle invenzioni: Dalla selce scheggiata al volo spaziali.* Edited with G. Zorzoli. Milan: Bompiani, 1961. Second edition, 1968.

*Opera aperta: Forma e indeterminazione nelle poetiche contemporanee.* (Includes *Le poetiche di Joyce.*) Milan: Bompiani, 1962. Revised edition, 1972.

*Diario minimo.* Milan: Mondadori, 1963. Second revised edition, 1976.

*Apocalittici e integrati: Comunicazioni di massa e teoria della cultura di massa.* Milan: Bompiani, 1964. Revised edition, 1977.

*Le poetiche di Joyce.* Milan: Bompiani, 1965. Second edition published as *Le poetiche di Joyce dalla "Summa" al "Finnegans Wake,"* 1966.

*Il caso Bond.* Edited with Oreste del Buono. Milan: Bompiani, 1965.

*La Bomba e il generale.* Illustrated by Eugenio Carmi. Milan: Bompiani, 1966. Revised edition, 1988.

*I tre cosmonauti.* Edited with Eugenio Carmi. Milan: Bompiani, 1966. Revised edition, 1988.

*Appunti per una semiologia delle comunicazioni visive.* Milan: Bompiani, 1967.

Introduction to *Noi vivi,* by Mimmo Castellano. Bari: Dedalo Libri, 1967.

*La struttura assente.* Milan: Bompiani, 1968. Revised edition, 1983.

*La definizione dell'arte.* Milan: Mursia, 1968.

*L'uomo e l'arte.* Vol. 1, *L'arte come mestiere.* Editor. Milan: Bompiani, 1969.

*I sistemi di segni e lo strutturalismo sovietico.* Edited with Remo Faccani. Milan: Bompiani, 1969. Second edition published as *Semiotica della letteratura in URSS,* 1974.

*L'Industria della cultura.* Editor. Milan: Bompiani, 1969.

*Dove e quando? Indagine sperimentale su due diverse edizioni di un servizio di "Almanacco."* Editor. Rome: RAI, 1969.

*Socialismo y consolacion: Reflexiones en torno a "Los misterios de Paris" de Eugene Sue.* Editor. Barcelona: Tusquets, 1970. Second edition, 1974.

*I fumetti di Mao.* Bari: Laterza, 1971.

*Le forme del contenuto.* Milan: Bompiani, 1971.

*Cent'anni dopo: Il ritorno dell'intreccio.* Edited with Cesare Sughi. Milan: Bompiani, 1971.

*Il segno.* Milan: Isedi, 1971. Second edition, Milan: Mondadori.

*I pampini bugiardi.* Edited with M. Bonazzi. Rimini: Guaraldi, 1972.

*Estetica e teoria dell'informazione.* Editor. Milan: Bompiani, 1972.

*Documenti su il nuovo medioevo.* Contributor. Milan: Bompiani, 1973.

*Eugenio Carmi: Una pittura de paesaggio?* Editor. Milan: G. Prearo, 1973.

*Il costume di casa: Evidenze e misteri dell'ideologia italiano.* Milan: Bompiani, 1973.

*Beato di Liebana: Miniature del Beato de Fernando I y Sancha.* Milan: Franco Maria Ricci, 1973.

*Il superuomo di massa: Studi sul romanzo popolare.* Rome: Cooperativa Scrittori, 1976. Revised edition, Milan: Bompiani, 1978.

*Storia di una rivoluzione mai esistita l'esperimento Vaduz.* Coeditor. Rome: RAI, 1976.

*Dalla periferia dell'Impero.* Milan: Bompiani, 1976.

*Come si fa una tesi di laurea.* Milan: Bompiani, 1977.

*Convegno su realta e ideologie dell'informazione.* Contributor. Milan, 1978; Milan: Il Saggiatore, 1979.

*Lector in fabula: La cooperazione interpretative nei testi narrativa.* Milan: Bompiani, 1979.

*Carolina Invernizio, Matilde Serao, Liala.* Contributor. Florence: Nuova Italia, 1979.

*Perche continuiamo a fare e a insegnare arte?* With others. Bologna: Cappelli, 1979.

*Il nome della rosa.* Milan: Bompiani, 1980.

*Postille a "Il nome della rosa."* Milan: Bompiani, 1983.

*Sette anni di desiderio.* Milan: Bompiani, 1983.

*Conceito de texto.* São Paulo: Queiroz, 1984.

*Sugli specchi e altri saggi.* Milan: Bompiani, 1985.

*Il pendolo di Foucault.* Milan: Bompiani, 1988.

*Lo strano caso della Hanau 1609.* Milan: Bompiani, 1989.

*I Limiti dell'interpretazione.* Milan: Bompiani, 1990.

*Stelle e stellette.* Genoa: Melangolo, 1991.

*Vocali.* Naples: Guida, 1991.

*Gli gnomi di gnu.* With Eugenio Carmi. Milan: Bompiani, 1992.

*Il Secondo diario minimo.* Milan: Bompiani, 1992.

*La ricerca della lingua perfetta nella cultura europea.* Bari: Laterza, 1993.

*L'Isola del giorno prima.* Milan: Bompiani, 1994.

*Povero Pinocchio.* Editor. N.p.: Comix, 1995.

# Bibliography

*Apocalyptic Spirituality*. Translated with an introduction by Bernard McGinn. Preface by Marjorie Reeves. New York: Paulist Press, 1979.

Blakney, Raymond Bernard. *Meister Eckhart: A Modern Translation*. New York: Harper and Brothers, 1941.

Bolton, W. F. *A History of Anglo-Latin Literature, 597–1066*. Princeton: Princeton University Press, 1967.

Bord, Janet. *Mazes and Labyrinths*. New York: Dutton, 1976.

Borges, Jorge Luis. *Dreamtigers*. Introduced by Miguel Enguidanos. Translated by Mildred Boyer and Harold Morland. Austin: University of Texas Press, 1964 and 1985.

———. *Labyrinths: Selected Stories and Other Writings*. Edited by Donald A. Yates and James E. Irby. Preface by André Maurois. New York: New Directions, 1962 and 1964.

Brown, Lloyd Arnold. *The Story of Maps*. New York: Dover Publications, 1979.

Cantor, Norman F. *The Civilization of the Middle Ages*. New York: HarperCollins, 1993.

Coletti, Theresa. *Naming the Rose: Eco, Medieval Signs, and Modern Theory*. Ithaca, New York: Cornell University Press, 1988.

Colish, Marcia L. *The Mirror of Language: A Study in the Medieval Theory of Knowledge*. Rev. ed. Lincoln: University of Nebraska, 1983.

Copleston, Frederick. *A History of Medieval Philosophy*. New York: Harper and Row, 1972.

———. *A History of Philosophy*. New rev. ed. 9 vols. New York: Doubleday, Image Books, 1985.

Cortinez, Carlos, ed. *Simply a Man of Letters: Panel Discussions and Papers from a Symposium on Jorge Luis Borges*. Orono: University of Maine at Orono Press, 1982.

Dahmus, Joseph Henry. *Dictionary of Medieval Civilization*. New York: Macmillan, 1984.

*Dictionary of Christian Biography, Literature, Sects and Doctrines*. Edited by Sir William Smith and Henry Wace. 4 vols. London: John Murray, 1877–1887. Reprinted, New York: AMS Press, 1974.

*Dictionary of Hymnology*. Edited by John Julian. Revised 2d ed. London: John Murray, 1915.

*Dictionary of the Middle Ages*. Editor in Chief, Joseph R. Strayer. 14 vols. New York: Scribner, 1982–1989.

Doob, Penelope Reed. *The Idea of the Labyrinth from Classical Antiquity through the Middle Ages*. Ithaca: Cornell University Press, 1990.

Durant, Will. *The Story of Civilization*. Vol. 4, *The Age of Faith: A History of Medieval Civilization—Christian, Islamic, and Judaic—From Constantine to Dante: A.D. 325–1300*. New York: Simon and Schuster, 1950.

Eckhart, Meister. *Die Deutschen Werke/Meister Eckhart*. Edited by Josef Quint. 5 vols. Stuttgart: W. Kohlhammer, 1958–1976.

——— *Die Lateinischen Werke/Meister Eckhart*. Edited by Joseph Koch et al. 6 vols. Stuttgart: W. Kohlhammer, 1936–.

Eliade, Mircea. *Images and Symbols: Studies in Religious Symbolism*. Translated by Philip Mairet. New York: Sheed and Ward, 1969.

Friedman, John Block. *The Monstrous Races in Medieval Art and Thought*. Cambridge: Harvard University Press, 1981.

Ganeri, Margherita. *"Il nome della rosa": una strategia di successo*. Introduction by Romano Luperini. Marina di Belvedere M.: Grisolia Editore, 1990.

Giles, John Allen. *The Complete Works of Venerable Bede, in the Original Latin*. 12 vols. London: Whittaker, 1843–1844.

Gilson, Étienne. *History of Christian Philosophy in the Middle Ages*. New York: Random House, 1955.

———. *The Spirit of Mediaeval Philosophy*. Translated by A. H. C. Downes. New York: Charles Scribner's Sons, 1940.

Haft, Adele. "Maps, Mazes, and Monsters: The Iconography of the Library in Umberto Eco's *The Name of the Rose*." *Studies in Iconography* 14 (1995): 9–50.

Harper, John. *The Forms and Orders of Western Liturgy from the Tenth to the Eighteenth Century*. New York: Oxford University Press, 1991.

Harvey, P. D. A. *Medieval Maps*. London: British Library, 1991.

Heilpern, John. "Out to Lunch," *Vanity Fair*, June 1984, 112.

*Hisperica Famina.* Vol. 1, *The A-Text.* Edited and translated by Michael W. Herren. Toronto: Pontifical Institute of Mediaeval Studies, 1974.

Hoyt, Edyth Viola Sage Armstrong. *Studies in the Apocalypse of John of Patmos.* 4th ed. Columbus, Ohio: Edwards Brothers, 1957.

Huizinga, Johan. *The Autumn of the Middle Ages.* Translated by Rodney J. Payton and Ulrich Mammitzsch. Chicago: University of Chicago Press, 1996.

Ickert, Klaus, and Ursula Schick. *Das Geheimnis der Rose—entschlüsselt (zu Umberto Ecos Weltbestseller "Der Name der Rose").* Munich: Wilhelm Heyne Verlag, 1986.

Inge, M. Thomas, ed. *Naming the Rose: Essays on Eco's "The Name of the Rose."* Jackson: University Press of Mississippi, 1988.

Kapsner, Oliver L. *A Benedictine Bibliography.* 2d ed. 2 vols. Collegeville, Minn.: St. John's Abbey Press, 1962. First supplement, Collegeville, Minn.: Liturgical Press, 1982.

Kettlewell, S. *Thomas à Kempis and the Brothers of Common Life.* 2 vols. New York: G. P. Putnam's Sons, 1882.

Lambert, Malcolm. *Franciscan Poverty: The Doctrine of the Absolute Poverty of Christ and the Apostles in the Franciscan Order, 1210–1323.* London: S. P. C. K., 1961.

Lea, Henry Charles. *History of the Inquisition of the Middle Ages.* 3 vols. New York: Macmillan, 1922.

Leff, Gordon. *Heresy in the Later Middle Ages: The Relation of Heterodoxy to Dissent, c.1250–c.1450.* 2 vols. Manchester: Manchester University Press, 1967.

Matthews, William Henry. *Mazes and Labyrinths.* London and New York: Longman, Green and Co., 1922.

McMurray, George R. *Jorge Luis Borges.* New York: Frederick Ungar, 1980.

*Middle Ages: A Concise Encyclopedia.* General Editor, H. R. Loyn. London: Thames and Hudson, 1989.

*New Catholic Encyclopedia.* Prepared by an editorial staff at the Catholic University of America. 17 vols. New York: McGraw-Hill, 1967–1979.

*New Grove Dictionary of Music and Musicians.* Edited by Stanley Sadie. 20 vols. Washington, D.C.: Grove's Dictionaries of Music, 1980.

Ohl, Raymond Theodore. *The Enigmas of Symphosius.* Ph. D. Diss., University of Pennsylvania, 1928.

*Oxford Classical Dictionary.* Edited by Simon Hornblower and Antony Spawforth. 3d ed. New York: Oxford University Press, 1996.

*Oxford Dictionary of the Christian Church.* Edited by E. A. Livingstone. 3d ed. New York: Oxford University Press, 1997.

*Oxford Illustrated History of Medieval Europe, The.* Edited by George Holmes. New York: Oxford University Press, 1988.

Ozment, Steven E. *The Age of Reform (1250–1550).* New Haven: Yale University Press, 1980.

Pischedda, Bruno. *Come leggere "Il nome della rosa."* Milan: Mursia, 1994.

Puletti, Ruggero. *"Il nome della rosa": struttura, forme e temi.* Manduria: Piero Lacaita Editore, 1995.

Raby, F. J. E. *A History of Christian-Latin Poetry from the Beginnings to the Close of the Middle Ages.* 2d ed. Oxford: Clarendon Press, 1953.

———. *A History of Secular Latin Poetry in the Middle Ages.* 2d ed. 2 vols. Oxford: Clarendon Press, 1957.

*Revelation.* Translated with introduction and commentary by J. Massyngberde Ford. The Anchor Bible, 38. Garden City, New York: Doubleday, 1975.

Rigg, A. G. *A History of Anglo-Latin Literature, 1066–1422.* New York: Cambridge University Press, 1992.

*Rule of St. Benedict in Latin and English.* Edited and translated by Abbot Justin McCann. London: B. Oates, 1952.

Seward, Barbara. *The Symbolic Rose.* New York: Columbia University Press, 1960.

Smalley, Beryl. *The Study of the Bible in the Middle Ages.* 3d ed. Oxford: Blackwell, 1983.

*Song of Songs.* Translated with introduction and commentary by Marvin H. Pope. The Anchor Bible, 7c. Garden City: Doubleday, 1977.

Thompson, James Westfall. *The Medieval Library.* Rev. ed. Chicago: University of Chicago Press, 1957.

*Toronto Medieval Bibliography* series. Toronto: University of Toronto Press, 1967–.

Wilford, John Noble. *The Mapmakers.* New York: Random House, 1981.

Woodward, David. "Medieval *Mappaemundi.*" In *The History of Cartography.* vol. 1, *Cartography in Prehistoric, Ancient, and Medieval Europe and the Mediterranean,* edited by J. B. Harley and David Woodward, 286–370. Chicago: University of Chicago Press, 1987.

# About the Authors

**Adele J. Haft** is an associate professor of Classics at Hunter College of the City University of New York. She has written about the *Iliad* and the *Odyssey*, presented papers in the United States and abroad, and taught at the Aegean Institute in Greece. After pursuing Homer's Odysseus and other tricksters through Greek poetry, she became entranced by world maps while researching *The Key to "The Name of the Rose."* She is currently writing a book on maps in twentieth-century poetry. Before coming to Hunter College in 1981, she taught at Princeton University, where she received her doctorate, and at University of Victoria in British Columbia, Canada. She resides in New York City with her husband, Canadian writer and historian, Jordan S. Zinovich.

**Jane G. White** is the Chairman of the Department of Foreign Languages at Dwight-Englewood School in Englewood, New Jersey, where she teaches Latin in grades 7–12. She has also taught the Classics at Trinity School, at Dickinson College, and, for seventeen years, in the Department of Classical and Oriental Studies of Hunter College. She received her doctorate in Classics from Yale University where she specialized in Latin poetry. Her academic interests include medieval Latin, Latin metrics, and the poetry of the Augustan Age. She is also the author of *Dinosaur Dot-to-Dots* (Weekly Reader, Field Publications), an educational activity book for young children.

**Robert J. White** is a professor in the Department of Classical and Oriental Studies of Hunter College, where he has taught since 1970. His doctorate in Classics is from Yale University, where he has also taught. He has lectured extensively—at the Smithsonian Institution, the Museum of Natural History, the Metropolitan Museum of Art, as well as at various American universities—on comparative mythology, secret languages of the Middle Ages, and the history of dream interpretation. His *Interpretation of Dreams: The Oneirocritica of Artemidorus* is the first English translation of the earliest complete manual on dream interpretation that survives from classical antiquity. Most recently, his book *An Avalanche of Anoraks (for People who Speak Foreign Languages Every Day . . . Whether They Know It or Not)* was published by Crown Trade Paperbacks in 1994.